Very Woman (

A Cerebral No

Remy de Gourmont

Alpha Editions

This edition published in 2024

ISBN : 9789362927668

Design and Setting By
Alpha Editions
www.alphaedis.com
Email - info@alphaedis.com

As per information held with us this book is in Public Domain.
This book is a reproduction of an important historical work. Alpha Editions uses the best technology to reproduce historical work in the same manner it was first published to preserve its original nature. Any marks or number seen are left intentionally to preserve its true form.

Contents

CHAPTER I	1
CHAPTER II	8
CHAPTER III	10
CHAPTER IV	15
CHAPTER V	18
CHAPTER VI	22
CHAPTER VII	27
CHAPTER VIII	30
CHAPTER IX	35
CHAPTER X	42
CHAPTER XI	46
CHAPTER XII	52
CHAPTER XIII	57
CHAPTER XIV	64
CHAPTER XV	70
CHAPTER XVI	75
CHAPTER XVII	80
CHAPTER XVIII	85
CHAPTER XIX	92
CHAPTER XX	98
CHAPTER XXI	102
CHAPTER XXII	109
CHAPTER XXIII	114
CHAPTER XXIV	117
CHAPTER XXV	123
CHAPTER XXVI	130

CHAPTER XXVII ....- 132 -
CHAPTER XXVIII ....- 134 -
CHAPTER XXIX ....- 139 -
CHAPTER XXX...- 143 -
CHAPTER XXXI ....- 146 -
CHAPTER XXXII ....- 149 -
CHAPTER XXXIII ....- 155 -
CHAPTER XXXIV ....- 161 -
CHAPTER XXXV...- 164 -
CHAPTER XXXVI ....- 166 -
CHAPTER XXXVII ....- 171 -
CHAPTER XXXVIII ....- 174 -
CHAPTER XXXIX ....- 178 -
CHAPTER XL ....- 183 -

CHAPTER I

THE DEAD LEAVES

"When Nature produces these masterpieces, she rarely offers them to the man who could best appreciate and be worthy of possessing them."
Kant: *Essay on the Beautiful*.

They walked side by side, under the gloomy old firs whose heavy branches leaned towards the yellowing lawn.

Countess Aubry, with her charm of a negotiator of worldly loves, had just hastily brought them together, as though they were predestined for each other.

They were slightly acquainted already. They remembered having met during the past winter in the Marigny Avenue Salon, that haunt of miscarried glories, and, during the past week that they had been staying at the Château de Rabodanges (among several invalids of distinction) they had succeeded in exchanging a few vaguely suggestive words, a few affected witticisms, not without disdain for such a vain communion.

The one knew that Madame Sixtine Magne, a widow, had never held out her neck towards a new necklace—and believed it. The other knew that Hubert d'Entragues had dedicated himself, by inclination rather than by necessity, to the imperious craft of a man of letters. Her first impulse had been to consider him a cavalry captain, but the name captivated her, that name faded in history, so far as a pretty woman was concerned, and which a young man restored to all its freshness, under her eyes. Amorous and royal reminiscences whose auricular remembrance had remained in her head like a viol sound, like ripplings on fading silks, and suddenly with rustlings of steel—an admission with which her preciosity amused itself, perhaps, for she was very artful, through pride.

Entragues, on his side, was at the point of confessing to the young woman that she dazzled his imagination, but he would have had to tell her at the same time the origin—too fantastic not to be futile—of this wound, and he feared to have the air of *inventing* a tale.

"Then," he reflected, "her mind would work, she would try to *please* me, forcing herself to deliberate charms. The experiment would be warped. I want to know what is in her; I want to penetrate coldly into the mysterious brambles of this sacred wood."

A man and a woman, at the age of useful deceits, are never cold or truthful, face to face. Hubert judged himself capable of acting naturally, but where does the natural begin with a being endowed with several spare souls? Sixtine was but half duped and, from the first words, let it be perceived.

"Are you familiar with all the emotions of a return?" asked Entragues. "It is delicious and torturing. You enter, agitated and unbalanced and, in the confusion of brief thoughts, you say to yourself: 'Can she be there! No, she is not there!' The fear of a sudden grief has anticipated the deception: can it be that such joys are attained outside of dreams? 'She is not there. *There is no danger.* What? No double lock? A night lamp? Is she there?' Yes, she was there, asleep in her rose-colored morning-gown; she had risen at the sound of the key and, with bare feet and disheveled hair, pale with emotion, kissed your face, whatever her eyes fell upon—lips, brow, nose, beard—one arm gently entwining itself about your neck, the other trembling at first with the hesitancy of not knowing where to rest. She cried, meanwhile, like a hallucinated person: 'It is you! It is you!' Then she stepped back to gaze at you, seemed to doubt, saying: 'Is it really you?' And she coyly gave herself to you, resting on your shoulder, gave herself again with an 'I am yours, still yours, as before!' You are thrilled with happiness. To depart leaving tears, to find a smile upon your return, a being transported by your presence—that is a real pleasure, mingled somewhat with that necessary vanity of feeling yourself indispensable to some one. A special vanity in which the male experiences a despotic satisfaction."

"Are you thus expected?" asked Sixtine.

"Who? I? No, but it might happen, and you see that I have felt it while talking to you. The slightest impulse diverts me from the present, the very tone of a voice rouses in me an inner activity and every possibility of life opens before me."

"You must be wonderful at pretending!"

"Ah, Madame," answered Entragues, "imagination does not destroy sincerity: it clothes sincerity with brocatels and rubies, places a diadem on it, but the same body of a woman is under the royal cloak, just as it is under tatters. To adorn truth is to respect it. This makes me recall those old evangelistaries that are so covered with illuminations that profane eyes seek the holy text in vain."

"There are difficult writings," said Sixtine.

"Divination is necessary when one cannot decipher. Have not women, the illiterates of love, all the intuitions of ignorance? Now then! if I said to you; 'The heart feels the heart's beating,' you would agree. We are still taken in by some old aphorisms."

"Nothing is so good as to let oneself be taken!"

Instantly astonished by a boldness of speech, whose precise meaning Entragues sought in her eyes, she laughed.

This purely voluntary laughter whose essence he notwithstanding penetrated, troubled him. A careful writer always on the quest for the exact word, new or old, rare or common, but of exact meaning, he imagined that everybody spoke as he himself wrote, when he wrote well. It was in good faith that he stubbornly persisted in reflecting, suddenly arrested by a disquietude in the presence of such words of conversation, habiliments of pure vanity. The knowledge of this eccentricity had never cured him of it, nor was he helped by the punishments of repeating this *mea culpa* after each mistake, taken from Goethe and composed for his personal use: "When he hears words, Entragues always believes there is a thought behind them."

This greatly complicated his life and his talks, inducing considerable hesitations in his replies, but he was concerned only with literary anatomy and he loved to encounter complex minds upon whose momentary intricacies he would later throw light, by deduction.

Since the nut might be empty, he threw a pebble at the tree so as to cause several others to fall.

"It is preferable to give than to be robbed."

"Oh!" Sixtine replied, "the sensation is quite different. First of all, not every one who wishes it, can be robbed. It is not even enough to let one's door ajar, Monsieur d'Entragues."

He felt that she had pronounced those last words in an insidious voice, but why? While waiting to understand, he responded:

"That itself would be quite a childish system. One usually places sentinels to guard the treasure chests and one provides locks for odd boxes. The spice in the pleasure of robbing lies in forcing, breaking, or taking a thing to pieces. True artists are repelled when there is nothing to do except thrust out the hand. But this is the most elementary ethics: no pleasure without effort."

"You are speaking of robbers, I of persons who are robbed. You can belong only to the one, I to the other class, the class that is at the mercy of an eventual rifling. I wanted to explain that it requires more than that the door should be ajar or, in fine, easy to open, for if one perfects the fastenings too thoroughly, the risk is taken of being assured a truly uncivil security. Well, more than all this, it is needful that there be visible or suspected objects to steal; it is needful that, by appearances, by external and attractive promises, the thief be tempted."

"You have anticipated me, Madame, in awarding yourself this personal compliment. I was about to make it. But you know, better than I do, your gifts and all that might draw curious and thievish hands to the dreamed of coffer."

"Too much frankness and irony, Monsieur d'Entragues. You were not born a thief."

"Alas! I have no hiding place secure enough for such larceny. My left hand would not know what to do with what my right hand pilfered."

The somewhat brutal candor of this disinterestedness did not seem to wound her. On the contrary, she thought:

"He is no fool. Another would have thrown himself at my imprudence, would instantly have urged me *to let myself be taken!*"

For his part, Hubert, seeing that the nuts were decidely meaty and not too tasteless, reflected:

"I will amuse myself again with throwing a few stones at the branches."

Sixtine forestalled him:

"What end are you aiming at? Love is too fleeting for your stability, let us admit. In that case, where does your life lead? Ah! poet, to success?"

"I am not a poet. I do not know how to cut my thoughts into little morsels that may be equal or unequal, according to the chance of the chopping knife. My prose gets its rhythm only through my breath. Only the pin thrusts of sensation mark its accents and the royal puerility of rich rhymes passes my understanding...."

The *vlouement* of a crow's wings agitated the air above the trees. Hubert remained silent, listening. Then:

"*Vlouement*, that's it, vlouement of wings, with the v v v. Is it the v v v or the f f f? The filement of wings? No, vlouement is better. Once more, crow!"

Sixtine, a trifle bewildered, stared at him open-mouthed.

"Those damned crow wings—one cannot describe them! Oh! success! Does the apple tree solicit applause for having borne fruit? From this one could construct quasi-evangelical parables. If I am not my own judge, and if I displease myself, what matter though I please others? Who are the others? Is there in the world an existence outside of myself? Possibly there is, but I am not aware of it. The world is myself, it owes me its existence, I have created it with my senses; it is my slave and no one else has any power over it. If we were thoroughly certain of the fact that nothing exists outside of ourselves, how prompt would be the cure of our vanities, how quickly our pleasures would be purged of it! Vanity is the fictive bond which links us to an imaginary exterior world. A little effort breaks it and we are free! Free, but lonely, lonely in the frightful solitude where we are born, where we live and die."

"What a sad philosophy, but what a proud one!"

"It contains less pride than sadness, and I would give much of its arrogance so as never to feel its bitterness."

"Who led you to it?" she queried, interested in these matters which seemed sufficiently new to her mind.

"But it is natural. How conceive a life different from what it clearly appears to eyes that can see? Yes! perhaps a certain illusion is possible.... What a pity, doubtless, what a pity for me that I did not meet you earlier—years ago. I would have loved you, and then...."

"What would have befallen your destiny, as a result?"

"You would have deluded me about life's value, Madame," Hubert continued, with a poetic enthusiasm that bordered on persiflage. "I would have drunk, like an external absinthe, the fluid illusion of your sea-green eyes and would have chained myself to life by the golden chain of your blond hair."

She veiled herself with indifference lightly embroidered with irony and, believing herself sheltered from a too inquisitive glance, ingenuously replied:

"It is really but three years since I was twenty-seven. It is now the thirtieth year, or almost."

He looked at her from head to foot, but without insolence.

"What frankness! But you have no need to lie." His eyes returned to her figure, which was a little full, he thought.

"Yes, esthetic, isn't it?" hazarded Sixtine, negligently lifting her arms to fasten some pin to her coiffure.

The gesture was fine and instrumental in making her bust more delicate in line.

He prudently replied:

"Esthetic? Oh, no! It seems good and with no treacheries."

A smile, quickly banished, attested the woman's contentment and was the most feminine efflorescence of the old human perversities. In a slow, undeceived voice, she said:

"It is lost time to wish to love me."

"See," Hubert returned, "you breathe on my bubbles and my sole and last chance of illusion vanishes, for in placing my desires in the past, I secretly constructed a bridge spanning the present. Ah! Madame, what transcendental cruelty!"

She was conscious of having taken a wretched crossroad, and of having become bemired there.

They spoke no more.

The shadow diffused itself in swift waves. Slightly nervous, Sixtine walked towards the light of a nearby glade, at the foot of the avenue. There, the oaks and beeches, whose foliage was already brightened by the setting sun, were grouped in a narrow grove. The wind passed, stirring the dry leaves. A low and heavy branch bent down with the sound of a rustling of stuffs. Like a drop of rain, a leaf, then many leaves, descended with a slow moaning sound.

"They follow me! They pursue me!" she cried, caught in the vortex she vainly fled.

And swept away, like a leaf in the circular flight of wind, she drew near Entragues, distracted, panting, crying all the time:

"The leaves pursue me, the dead leaves pursue me!"

"What is the matter," Hubert asked, surprised by such a strange crisis.

While, still frantic and trembling, she seized his arm and leaned against it, he coldly added:

"Have you ever committed a crime in your life?"

This ironic interrogation changed the nature of the fever, like scalding water on a stone.

"Perhaps!" she answered, suddenly pale.

"Then you become altogether interesting."

It was beyond her strength to retort to this impertinence. With a trembling of all her little muscles, and without knowing why she did it, she tried to pull off her gloves. When one of her hands was free, she shook it, pulled it, cracked its joints.

"Excuse me," Entragues continued. He took a malicious pleasure in making the untuned instrument vibrate. "But is there not a stain on the little finger?"

"No, it was the poison."

This came from her lips with the calmness of a meditated confession.

His eyes sincerely troubled, Hubert watched the monster who disengaged herself and fled, throwing these words to him as an adieu:

"I am leaving tomorrow, come to see me."

CHAPTER II

MADAME DU BOYS

"... Quid agunt in corpore casto Cerussa
et minium, centumque venena colorum?
Mentis honor morumque decus sunt vincula
Conjugii...."
(Sancti Claudius Marius Victor,
De perversis suae aetatis moribus)

Hubert had left Rabodanges a few days after Sixtine's departure. The unvaried green of the fields saddened him and, despite the ingenuity of the countess, deprived of the company of the young woman who puzzled him to the utmost, the château seemed to him as though plunged in a funereal widowhood.

He did not even execute his plans of visiting the Mortagne Trappists, but took the train and entered Paris one evening in a state of real satisfaction.

For him, Paris was neither the streets nor the boulevards and theaters. Paris, for Entragues, was confined within the somewhat narrow bounds of his study, peopled with pleasant phantoms of his imagination. There, sad and vague beings, pensive and formless, stirred restlessly, imploring existence, Entragues lived with them in an almost disquieting familiarity. He beheld them, heard them, repaired with them to whatever sphere their activity necessitated. In short, he underwent the keenest phenomena of hallucination.

Thus it was that, on the morrow of his return, Madame du Boys came to occupy him with her adventures. It was a matter of reconciling her in a logical way with her husband whom she had abandoned, to follow to Geneva a Polish count, retired there after sundry nihilistic adventures. Artémise du Boys was how she spelled her name after her adulterous lark, the while her husband, secretary-cashier of the *Union de la Bonne-Science*, the simple Monsieur Dubois, bewailed his irreparable misfortune.

He groaned and Madame du Boys grew bored, an excellent occasion for once more renewing the bond and putting into practice several verses from the Gospels. Irreparable? And the pardon? One was on the point of agreeing to ask it, the other waited for her to force his hand.

"Ah! Madame du Boys," mused Entragues, gazing upon his fair visitor, "You do not know your husband. Write to him again. Just say: 'I was a little lark of a woman and I was lured away!' Repeat this simple idea through four beautiful pages in a tiny slanting handwriting that trembles and is steeped in tears (Oh! but true tears, scientific tears, acidulated and proportioned with the desired salt of grief),—do this, O my love, and you will see."

Without awaiting her reply, and while Madame du Boys meditated, a modest and very agreeable sinner, Entragues went to comfort the secretary of the *Bonne-Science*. A simple and quite suitable office: journals, brochures, registers, a general list of the founding members, patrons, donors, residents, foreigners, honorary members, orders depending on the results of preliminary payments, sums deposited, sums due, and different titles.

"You are sad? Yes, a broken life. But, Monsieur Dubois, all lives are broken, just as all sticks thrown in the water are broken. Existence bends souls, we are not made for life. A deception gives it to us, trickery conserves it for us. Ah! I know that philosophy is not your forte; neither founder nor patron, nothing but an appointed secretary. If you are not a philosopher, why did you marry such a pretty woman as Madame du Boys? Only a philosopher could be justified in committing such imprudences, for he knows how to make an abstraction at the proper time. Figures have taught you other duties. Everything is calculated on the register page, and what is absent is called memory. Isn't it the pure truth, stripped of all symbols, that you still love her? Act as a Christian, not as a coward enslaved to habits. So! you have charge of this weak soul and you should, like the Good Shepherd, bear her on your shoulders and save her from the devouring lion. But why do you not go after her, since she has lost her way? Pride chains you to your books. You think you are a Christian, but you are a stoic. Monsieur Dubois, modern Good Shepherds use railroads and telegraphs without shame. Go! Ah! the donors? Well, telegraph! No, it is at least necessary that the sinful sheep go half way, that the sinner behave like a Magdalene and weep. Well, I will bring her to you. Thus, your wife left you to follow her pleasure; she returns somewhat atremble, but confident, and you will pardon her? Will you open your door to her, your arms, your bed? Will you write 'Memory' in the debit side of past days, under days of marital solitude, meaning, in this instance, oblivion. And will the first repast together be a holiday feast, and the first night together a night of happiness? You will do all this, Monsieur Dubois, because you are a Christian and not a stoic. I slandered you. And you will tell me of the interview, of the noble pardon, in low tones for my personal edification, and I will be able to narrate it, aloud, for the edification of the age?"

Having ended these reveries, Entragues, to amuse himself, recopied in ink the note book leaves on which he had scribbled while on the train, during evenings, in his bed, during mornings, or in the solitude of the avenues.

CHAPTER III

TRAVEL NOTES

Rai-Aube

"And when you will be thus formed, when
you will be imbued with this truth, 'there
is no truth, nothing truly existent for you
except what your fertile mind gives,' observe
the general course of the world and, letting
it follow its own way, associate with the
minority."
Goethe: *Testament*.

Dreux.—To see trains pass by—to see life pass by—never to go within save to strike cushions.

A little farther.—Trains have a destination; life has none. But life's originality lies precisely in having no destination. I occasionally find in it, as in old lace, the same charm of uselessness.

A little farther.—I viewed the landscape as far as Dreux. The unconsciousness of the vegetable kingdom is a decidedly too melancholy void. To become interested in it, one must make it live by incorporating oneself with the trees and grass, transferring the sentient soul of a man into the oak's trunk. I am an oak, I am a holly-tree, I am a wild poppy, but I realize it, while the oak, the holly-tree, the wild poppy do not: for this reason they do not exist. Pantheists are very fine fellows.

Nonancourt.—These syllables shouted through the train evoke a pretty convent of nuns, rather dissolute before the reform of Borromée; afterwards, it was devoted to God until the revolutionary dispersal. Now the house, henceforth plebeian, serves as a barn, stable and pigsty. As the notary who last sold it said: "It will serve as a farm." Cows now ruminate where women once prayed—a notable advance.

Tillières.—A ravine cuts this plain in two, a dastardly act, life.

Verneuil.—I was alone since leaving Paris. A man enters, opens his newspaper and expands into a *gauloiserie*. If it were evening, near his better half, or if, in my place, some obliging girl revealed a part of her foot! These flights of animalism are truly painful to a calm man. The flower-like opening contracts; the joyous flame of eyes brightens into a waxing ferocity; cruel lust opens its mouth and shows its teeth. Awaking: a searching glance: the mimicry by degrees is extinguished and there remains the disappointed ennui of a vain excitement. No, I do not care to serve as an aphrodisiac to citizens. To think of this would compel you towards a monachal literature, hard and contemptuous of vile lust.

Bourth or nearby.—The man speaks. It was inevitable. He speaks of himself, full of a need of making himself known, of introducing the passerby into his little universe. He travels for a bookseller of religious books. He goes from parsonage to parsonage, well received by the *curés*, who ask him to dinner. A good clientele and good payers. His center is Verneuil; thence he radiates, like an apostle. Usually a horse and carriage, rented for the season, conducts him from church to church; having some business to transact at Laigle, he took a train to amuse himself; to amuse himself he climbed into a first-class apartment with a second-class ticket. (There is no inspection at such hours.) "Verneuil's a fine town. A rare thing for the province (isn't it so, between ourselves), that this big borough has a well-kept inn, quite renovated." He is a free-thinker, but tolerant, enveloping with the same sympathetic pity, children, women, priests, devout souls—more stupid than ill-meaning, he assures you. As for himself, if a God exists he will go straight to Heaven, never having hurt a fly. Sound instruction will gradually cure us of religion. He has no fear on this score and, his conscience quite tranquil, places his *Corneille de la Pierre* for the best. Unmarried, but desiring a marriage so as to have sturdy little republicans, strong defenders of *la Patrie*. Alsace and Lorraine, Gambetta, and so forth.

Laigle.—He offers me *something*. I politely decline, he withdraws. Throughout the world, this matter interests the millions of similarly constituted minds: for whom do you work, poor unconscious bees? The species? But does the intelligence of a few balance the universal stupidity?

Rai-Aube.—A village I never again shall see, a village with such a pretty name, with such a fine combination of radiant words—aurora and ray—an alliance of syllables married by a morning smile; grasses watered by the freshness of dew, transparent springs, murmuring fluidity of waters flowing under the abundant rushes: all this, Rai-Aube, and oblivion, and the ineffable, palpitates in the white letters of your name, alluring and fugitive rebus hung on the gable of the station! Remembrance rather than vision: in my youth I lived among these vernal delights and steeped myself in them. I do not belong to towns and a built-up plot of ground does not incite me to excessive joys. All that was created by youthful eyes remains young, and for me the countryside often has the sex of its spelling, even under the surplice of snow. That alone remains of my earliest years: all is dead, whether by real death or the death of memory. The tenderness of vague figures bending towards my precocious orphanhood, is the farthest removed; of school, the horror is still painful to remember; a Dantesque and futile horror inflicted upon my pitiful childhood. But already, due a little to my will, the world retreated from me and by a slow or sudden recreation, I reformed for myself a life more harmonious with my intimate sense. But already, in arrogant moments, I scorned everything external to me, everything that had not been reformed and reground by the machine ceaselessly in motion in my head. Excepting the unknowable principle, I have fashioned everything anew; at least, for scepticism even gnaws at one's personality, such is the allusion in which I have confined myself.

With such a fixed determination, with this Kantian system which can be called transcendental egoism, my life has marched with a relatively light pace. Of all the griefs which my will has not succeeded in putting aside, the heaviest to bear is my very solitude. Never having surrendered to its deceits, I know not if hope be aught but a bleeding spur, driving man towards a future nothingness. I know not if the wound opened without respite and the sight of the spilled blood be not powerful stimulants necessary for the functioning of the human mechanism. I have never experienced them. I only believe in the final charnel-house, but without coveting it. Life does not yet displease me sufficiently. Without this, having no philosophical principles to converge with a possible practice, I would be consistent with my disgust and would give it my sanction. Like Crantor, I will die "without being astonished;" if my organs are still sound when death comes, perhaps regretfully. As for survival, on this point I have no such tranquilizing ideas as has the traveling salesman of Dreux. Perhaps the delightful Unconscious reserves some of its good tricks for the truly supreme, last moment of corporeal decomposition! This relative fear doubtless comes to me from my Christian youth, and I repudiate neither the one nor the other; Catholicism is an aristocracy. I do not know how this positive religion can come to be allied in me with subjective idealism; it is an obscure amalgam, like all heresies. Theology always procured me the most agreeable reading; from Augustine I can go to Claudius Mamertinus; there the joys are not less because of the curiosity. How I would have loved to be a bishop in some less modern Rome, or a cardinal! If I dwelt on this rather sterile desire, a sensation of a deficient life would clutch my throat, a vulgar sensation that my pride contemptuously repels. And then, have I not of my own accord tasted the mystic happiness and the celestial anguishes of episcopacy? Have I not clothed myself with the violet robe lifted at the bottom, or trailing up the stairs of the altar? Have I not ascended, mitre on head, the steps of the presidial chair? What then would reality serve me, when I have the dream and the faculty of changing myself like Proteus, the faculty of successively possessing all forms of life, all states of soul which man diversifies himself.

Surdon.—Curled feathers bob up and plunge into the window. Seeing me alone, the female traveler hesitates, but the whistle has blown, a guard shoves her inside. She sits down opposite me, fallen there somewhat out of breath; she is uneasy although she is not blushing. The hesitation came from the fear of appearing to have expressly chosen the compartment in which sat one man. I try to reassure her with very polished phrases, but I succeed imperfectly. I am quite certain that some good proverb would amuse and pique her. I end with: "Occasion makes the thief." In the province, proverbs, that grammatical archæology, are still the current coin of conversation; they permit the saying of nothing at all while appearing to say a great deal. She appreciated my adage and complained of the habitual grossness of men. I answer her: "That is because women always desire what is not offered them and scorn what is offered them. A delicate man, by indefinable signs, lets his fancy be guessed, and does not commit himself to a decisive movement until the exact moment when he sees that it is shared." She smiles: "How does one feel this?" I answer: "The acquiescences are diverse, but there is a special flicker of the eye-lashes, very slow, which it is difficult to mistake." She looks at me with astonishment. A very honest woman, amused at this scabrous conversation, but inexperienced. Her youth and the rosiness of her complexion bespeak a recent marriage and little maternity: openly curious, having an eternity of ten years before her, to learn the secret. Otherwise pretty, and with much distinction, that modern name for grace; between blonde and brunette; clear, rather large eyes, the lower part of her face having no hint of brutishness. The trip from Surdon to Argentan takes sixteen minutes; our several questions and replies have exhausted them. The brake is put on, we slow up. Before I could anticipate her movement, she opens the carriage door until the train comes to a stop, holds the door back, and there I am, surprised to receive, at the same time, an equivocal bow and a glance of surprising intensity.

Is it an invitation to run after her? I believe it is and I hasten out, but I cannot find her. I had rapidly taken my light hand baggage, valise, rug, overcoat, etc. I am not forced to return to my railway carriage and I leave the station to seek the carriage bearing the arms of the countess. She is waiting for me and, thank heaven! I am the only one expected to-day. I will travel *tête-à-tête* with my disappointment. The coachman said the trip would take an hour, I have an hour in which to school myself with such a useless emotion. We start off; here is the Orne with its two adjacent bridges and, along the stream embanked with walls, an amusing house with balustrades and balconies on the water; an umbrella shop with a strolling singer's good-looking red parasol for an emblem; not a carriage in the peaceful streets, and thus one leads to doors of men and women, but not children; the birdless cage, the childless home: it was a prophecy. The school, the college, the barracks, the office, the study: the French revolution has perfected slavery, it is unanimous. A half-

Gothic church, some old gables and less uniform façades amuse me; but we go quickly, despite the climb; then the sorry outskirts, the flat road, the stretch of grey level grass, race-grounds and wheels, some poplars.

CHAPTER IV

REFLECTIONS

"In carne enim ambulantes non secundum
carnem militamus."
Saint Paul, *Cor.*, II, 10, 3.

Entragues wrote only in the morning, but often extended his work of the forenoon into the afternoon. When he did not feel lucid enough for the logic of prose, he amused himself. Poetry, a simple music admitting neither passion nor analysis, is only intended to suggest vague sentiments and confused sensations; a half-consciousness suffices for it. In imitation of Saint Notker, he composed obscure sequences full of alliterations and interior assonances. Walt Whitman, with his intuitive genius, unconsciously restored this lost poetic form. Entragues, at certain hours, delighted in it. This literature of about the tenth century, usually judged as the puerile distraction of barbarous monks, seemed to him on the contrary full of an ingenuous freshness and of an ingenious refinement. Notker charmed him, besides, by the red-blooded boldness of his metaphors, charmed and terrified him while throwing him on his knees before this God for whom prayer is a bleeding holocaust, and who demands, like a slaughtering of lambs, "immolated praise." He also took pleasure in a short and delicate sequence of Godeschalk, where Saint Mary Magdalene "covers with kisses" the feet of Jesus "which she has washed with her tears." A monk of the eleventh century had written a work entitled: *The Nothingness in the Darkness*. Entragues could find no trace of it beyond the mention of the title. It was one of the unknown books he would have liked to read.

Apart from two or three scorners of actual life, a strict logician of criticism, an extreme and absolute dreamer, an extraordinary creator of phrases and shaper of images, and several modern poets, he now hardly ever opened anything but antique theologies and dictionaries. He had a mania for lexicons, tools which seemed to him, generally, more interesting than works, and he spent over such instruments, often quite useless, many an idle hour. Thus ended the first day of his return.

On the morrow, after a night in which he had relived some of the most characteristic minutes passed with Sixtine at the château de Rabodanges, Hubert suspected that his life was about to change in orientation, that an inevitable crisis threatened him. It was a propitious occasion for meditation. In several weeks perhaps—oh! only perhaps!—he will have undergone obvious modifications. It was necessary—in order to make a reckoning of it later—to note certain dominant traits of the state of his actual mind, to proceed to a summary examination of consciousness. His travel note book already containing some sufficiently precise remarks on this subject, he restricted himself to completing them with the following reflections:

"I am ashamed to admit it, so banal is this malady: I am bored. I have excruciating awakenings. I believe in nothing and I do not love. My calling is a sad one. It is to experiment with all the griefs and all the horrors of the human soul, so that men may recognize themselves in my work and say: 'Well roared, lion'! Yet, I am free: without nightly obligations, neither a parasite nor a worldling, nor a dramatic critic, I retire early, when I please. Having reached my thirtieth year with hardly any social relations, having enough revenue to be independent, I act in everything as I desire, heedless of general customs and satisfied, for example, to testify my scorn for the civilization of gas, by burning my lamp for ten hours. I am free, I have neither wife nor mistress. I fear mistresses for the confusion in which they throw the regularity of my work; but with sensitive beings a large lagoon is hollowed from principles to acts. When I am with some one, I desire solitude; alone, I feel the disquietudes of the void.

"When the commandment of the flesh hurls me to lustful adorations, I blush at such a servitude and at the earliest lucid moment I treat myself with contempt. When I have long stored the concentrated poison of vain seeds, hammer strokes drum on me, my organism gives way and my brain becomes troubled. Never having been kept upright by hair-cloth, iron tacks, wounds freshened by perpetual excoriations, pitiless fasts, privation of sleep, nor any of the mystic and Franciscan maneuvers, I subdue my flesh by leading it to pasture, but with no more sin in my intention than an invalid who breaks his abstinence to procure a remedy. Although pleasure follows, it is an obedience to the ineluctable commands governing animated life. Though I accept it, it is a human weakness. To love so much that one wishes to die—that test I have had in adolescence, and the reasonable insensibility of the woman I adored has never shed any bitterness on that far off remembrance. I do not smile pityingly on these days of umbrageous follies. After ten or eleven years, I am as sure as I was at the first hour of having been deprived of the greatest happiness put within reach of my hands by the Decrees, and in moments of emotion this regret can still throw a gloom over my revery. Since then, nothing but transitory pluckings; barely, now and then, an attempt at the band broken at the first touch.

"Far from being the aim of my life, sensation is its accident: I reserve my voluntary strength for the tales I tell my contemporaries. They have been found cold and ironic, but I have neither the quality to be an enthusiast of my age, nor to take it too seriously. Another motive removes me from emotional researches: without being a pessimist, without denying the possibility of satisfaction, without even denying happiness, I scorn it. I do not seek to aggravate my miseries by meditations on the universal misery, to which my egoism, moreover, makes me almost indifferent. A state of perfect peace of mind agrees with me. It is possible for me to regret an unhatched joy, but I wish neither to provoke nor to lie in wait for the hatching. In fine, there is no doubt that I do not know how to live. A perpetual celebration, my existence is the very negation of ordinary life, which is composed of ordinary loves. I have no tendency towards the altruisms demanded by society. If ever I could be drawn from myself, for the benefit of some creation, it would be in the manner of an imaginative person, at all points re-creating the object of my passion, minutely scrutinizing the mechanism of my impressions. Such is my character: it is obvious that I have not applied myself to elude the knowledge of myself; and yet no one knows better than I do to what point this knowledge is puerile and unhealthy."

CHAPTER V

MORE TRAVEL NOTES

The Pale and Green Moon

"In hac hora anima ebria videtur,
Ut amoris stimulis magis perforetur."
Saint Bonaventure, Philomena.

Château de Rabodanges, in the portrait chamber, September 12.—Upon arriving, I was received by Henri de Fortier, director of *la Revue spéculative*, and Michel Paysant, whose novels, full of swelling busts and caressing glances, charm families which mistake impotence for chastity. Fortier mentions the names of the guests to me. None of my acquaintances are here. Separated from the general, her husband, Countess Aubry brings to the country, at the summer end, her cosmopolitan salon which is frequented by the grand courtiers of academic or worldly literature. It is rumored that Fortier succeeds, in her gallant nights, the Bonapartist deputy who recently died and with whom she had an open liaison. Fortier assumes the modest airs of a host. At the dinner, several aristocrats who live in the vicinity mention the fact that the hunting season has opened. The only interesting face to see is that of a young fair woman, with sparkling eyes, who is either silent or speaks to Madame Aubry alone. A stroll in the moonlight follows, then the neighbors call for their carriages. Fortier disappears with the countess. Paysant takes my arm and prattles.

He groans over his vexations as a chief clerk of literature. Just now he would like to rest, even to loaf, but a week does not pass without some publisher, old or young, coming to entreat of him a volume to restore his business or launch his bookshop. Accordingly, his repressed Gallic nature would freely awake and he would write several jolly stories. But the unity of his work! That would no longer turn out to be Paysant, and the Academy would perhaps knit its brow. He attempts a laugh, but one feels an apprehensive reverence within the depths of his deferential brain. A silence, and he greedily describes the young woman I had noticed. The technique of the patrician gives to his eloquence a disinterested tone, but one divines the wet mouth and the hand, with kneading gestures, caressing the absent forms. I maintain that women are neither beautiful nor ugly, and that their whole charm radiates from their sex: desire sketches beauty and love completes it. A certain ugly creature, in the vulgar sense of the word, has been able to assume an ideal beauty, while another woman, by all judged admirable, has not passed beyond the limbo of a rough draught, never having been loved. Paysant shouts this paradox: feminine beauty is real and independent of sentiment. She is capable of feeling, yes? Doubtless, that is a special pleasure, yes, a special one. By adroitly goading him, one could make him confess his tastes of a fondler, of a senile love of touching, but I know not why, I am afraid lest his pathology take up Madame Sixtine as a subject of demonstration.

We return to the château. Everybody has surrendered to the rare pleasure of retiring early. Only Fortier awaits us, to conduct me to my room. It seems that a friend of the countess is enthusiastic about the *Revue spéculative* and is going to espouse it under a dotal system, making it an allowance of fifty thousand francs, which it lacks. This Fortier has a mania for offering incomprehensible metaphors.

"Some one is going to put fifty thousand francs into the *Revue*!"

"Precisely."

"And you will become?"

"Editor in chief instead of director."

"And the director?"

"A pseudonym." I know Fortier; he will not take offense.

"Now, confess that it is the countess." He smiles and immediately gallops across the faded fields of the dithyramb:

"She is charming, generous, devoted to art, and without personal ambition."

"Except to be loved?"

"I charge myself with that."

This unconstraint interests my natural curiosity, and with little contradictions powdered with some skepticism, I excite him to the point where he tells me everything. He was presented by Malaval, who remarked that his elegance of a clipped dog would turn the head of the countess. It was an embarrassing introduction, but Fortier showed wit—so he claims. There followed allurements, sly winks, the habit of quarreling with each other, an absence, several letters wherein a light tenderness fluttered. She was alone when he returned. Without speech, their arms outstretched—there they were, trembling and lovers. Fortier is incapable of inventing and, perhaps, of lying. He even has the air of finding this natural and fatal. It had to happen.

"Is it not so?"

"Doubtless."

I take leave of him. Before departing, he asks me to furnish some pages for the first number of *la Spéculative*, new series. This line finished, I go to sleep, but why is this room called the portrait chamber?

September 13, morning.—I have dreamed of this portrait and I seek it in every corner, in every section of the walls. The room is quite remarkably bare: a uniform gray paper; above the Empire fireplace, a looking glass which reaches to the ceiling; the bed occupies one of the sides of the floor; to the right of the door, a bookcase contains some old books; to the left is a chest of drawers topped with a new mirror; opposite are two windows; between the two windows, a dressing table and another glass. Nothing else.

September 14, evening.—We took an excursion to Roches-Noires. Monsieur B——, who was our guide, killed a snake with a few blows of a little stick. Then, Madame Magne took the reptile and in an instant made a bracelet of the still moving creature. The countess uttered a cry, the viper had to be thrown into a hole, and I reflected upon the biblical and singular sympathy between women and serpents, for the countess cried without sincerity and Madame de B——. pitied the poor creature of the good Lord.

September 14, morning.—I have seen the portrait. The pale and green moon soared into my room. I had just awakened, and obscure and ophidian visions still haunted me. With feverish eyes I distrustfully gazed around me, while logical and absurd reasonings multiplied in my head, their fugacity leaving me with a doubt as to the precise place of my actual existence. Was I in the midst of the brambles and precipices of Roches-Noire? No. Was I in my room, and in my bed, far from the vipers and grimacing stones? Perhaps. See! above the mantlepiece the mirror slowly changes its tint: its lunar green, its green of transparent waters underneath beeches, brightens and grows golden. One would say that in the center of the glimmering, as on the moon's very face, shadows with human features project, while above the vague figure there winds a luminous undulation like loosened and floating blond hair. Without being able to analyze the rest of the sudden transformation, I see it, in the twinkling of an eye, completed. Clear and animate, the portrait gazes on me; it is, feature for feature, that of the woman with the reptile. For several moments, long and unforgettable moments, the vision grew resplendent, then it vanished, as though by a breath.

September 15, morning.—I awoke at the same hour, but the mirror remained green and I did not see the portrait again. I think of nothing but this. All day yesterday, while Madame Sixtine Magne was with us, I looked at her; when she was no longer there, I evoked her.

September 15, evening.—The countess quickly questioned me, while we were on the bank of the Orne: "By the way, did you see the portrait? No, for you would have said so. Besides, to see it one must now, it seems, be endowed with a certain mystery. It is a trick sometimes played upon easily troubled imaginations. There is a history. Monsieur de B——. tells it very well. Make him discuss this chapter after dinner." I could not find a word to answer. I have seen the portrait, but how proceed to boast of that privilege? The angling for crawfish continues; I am asked to take part in it. In a frame of leaves, under the silvered alders, the young woman, who henceforth has rights to interest me, seems passionately absorbed in a book whose pages she cuts with her finger. Monsieur de B——. could not remain for dinner and no one has spoken again of the portrait chamber. So much the better....

(End of the Travel Notes).—There, in fact, ended the scribbled pages, Hubert having betaken himself to dream of his impressions instead of transcribing them. He did not wish to write them down too late, without some necessary preliminary moments, so as not to take the risk of confounding the chronology of the little things whose logical order is of prime importance. The remainder of the notebook was white. Yet when he perused them later, he perceived a sheet of loose paper where could be traced some intentions of poetry. This more narrowly fixed his thoughts upon Sixtine: it was truly with her that he was concerned in his prose, in his verses, in his life.

CHAPTER VI

DREAM FIGURE

"O Créateur de l'universel monde,
Ma pauvre âme est troublée grandement!"
Heures *à l'usaige de Paris*, 1488.

Sixtine was far from him, and yet he believed that he saw her nearby.

All afternoon he preserved the illusion of walking in her company. She suddenly appeared in a dress of changing colors: the cloth, a light and pale green silk, had golden clasps. Her shoes made no sound; her smile, instead of speech, and diverse inflexions of her muscles, expressed her thoughts; nevertheless, but only once, he positively heard the sound of her voice. "So you would like me to tell you the history of the portrait chamber?" Preoccupied in establishing the fundamental sound of the recovered sequence which for an instant tyrannized him, Entragues listened to the question without immediately perceiving its sense. He was going to reply and agree, but Sixtine, under the parasol which she had opened, was reading and he dared not disturb her. The parasol, too, by its oddness, caused his mind to wander. It was of such limpid and transparent yellow that through it he beheld, barely shaded by a luminous shadow, the shoulders of Sixtine and her head bent upon the book.

They walked along the quay, from the rue du Bac, where he had begun to feel her presence, to the Saint-Michel Square. The charming, shining Seine was iridescent with the play of oblique rays striking against its current; sparkling foam fell on the prows; the fringe of the bank was dotted with sails on which a keen wind played; the canvas crackled like flames; the lines of anchored boats here and there rumbled under the shock; the multicolored parapets retreated.

Entragues bought no lexicon; he looked at the serried backs of books, without even reading the black or golden titles.

In a deserted spot, along the wooden balustrade, and as the first gas light flickered in a *café*, he was accosted by a young man who passed as a poet, perhaps because of the rare beauty of his face.

"How singular! You are alone, yet one would swear that an invisible person accompanied you."

"I am now alone, my dear Sanglade."

Sixtine, in fact, had just disappeared from Entragues sight and Sanglade had the impression of having awkwardly interrupted a *tête-à-tête*, an impression that was quite metaphorical, for with an air of bantering timidity, he added:

"You are seeking rhymes. I will give you some, I have them all at my command. Without this gift, I would not be a poet."

"Yes, without this you *would* be a poet."

"In prose, perhaps," answered Sanglade, "but in verse?"

Entragues purposely let him run on, having no mind for esthetic tournaments. They went up the boulevard. At the Luxembourg, Sanglade, tired of discoursing in monologue, took advantage of a passing friend and returned. Entragues made for a quiet *café*, protected with carpets, where his horror of sound could readily be satisfied.

Since his return, save for a brief interview on the first morning, he had been able to abstract Sixtine from his immediate thoughts. It was with a perfect coldness that he had recopied into good French his brief travel notes where, towards the end, the name of this woman, hardly known, recurred with each verse, like an amen. But, and here he recognized the occult power of words, the material transcription of those syllables had acted violently on his imagination. He had lived whole hours with her, and now that the mystic power of the vision was spent, he still thought of the absent one.

"She must have gone to Bagnoles for one of those imaginary illnesses which women never think of treating save in their periods of boredom. Restless or bored: she had these two states in almost equal doses. Then if her head is troubled with love, she will not experience it until the time when one questions oneself: uncertain questions, uncertain answers! And boredom? To explain it, you must admit that the advance or recoil of this dawning caprice has nothing to do with her will and that she may be unconscious of her own sentiment. That is it: she loves, therefore the uneasiness; but she does not know it, therefore the ennui. It is necessary to note this. Could she have returned?"

Hubert believed himself merely touched by a simple analytical fever. Often, for the sole pleasure of taking stock with himself, he had followed, in their psychic evolutions, many interesting subjects; of women, particularly, but deceived by a consideration of the inscrutable motive, they had divined another one and had begun to simper at the investigator. Thus it used to end, whether Entragues digressed, or whether a series led him into a secret laboratory experiment.

Even in this last case, it was short, for he had hardly ever tried his tests except upon vile souls often belonging to prostituted organisms.

Sixtine was of the caste numbered one or two, coming from an aristocratic convent and from an idle leisurely family.

Nothing certain at the first approach, because of the modern confusion and personal reclassification, but fallen rather than parvenu, belonging at least to those who cultivate a relative leisure in an avowed independence. As for certain other problems which puzzled him, he would amuse himself in resolving them gradually, at her home, with the aid of subtle questions, for he meant to accept her invitation and would go to see her.

Such a minute revery denoted a certain possession. Entragues did not yet suspect, or perhaps did not wish to condescend to admit to himself that the agreeable and feminine form of mystery acted on his imagination more than on his curiosity.

Sixtine was graceful and her contours corresponded with the harmony requisite to evoke the word of beauty. Blond her hair, and a golden green, her eyes; violent the mouth and exquisitely white, her teeth! Ah! the violent mouth broke the harmony, a cold esthetician would have said, but, and this was the proof that Hubert already was a prey to desire, he loved its destructive violence, seeing it in but a more assured promise of pleasure. Just then Entragues gave such a sharp start that the gamblers close to him held the dice-box sus-about to make. The dice rattled in the copper box pended in air, and suppressed the bets they were and Entragues reflected on his nerves.

"It was because of the ambiguity, that was the cause, my soul! The ambiguity threw the poison."

"Oh! was he going to take as a serious confession idle words playfully uttered on the wings of a causerie. This time, was it not really the old malady of chimerical fancies? He smiled at himself, and almost grew out of patience. Ah! the thing was not to accuse her because of a confession, not to reveal himself as devoid of criticism as a public accuser, but not to deny her criminal potentiality. What a doll full of bran instead of blood, seamed with threads instead of nerves, is a woman incapable of crime! As well say that she is incapable of passion! Our cowardly civilization, itself, absolves the bloody consequences of love, sparing such women the futile expiation of an inevitable act. The equivocation he had read on Sixtine's face was the mark of election, the sign of possible passion, the proof that she was a woman."

This deduction reassured Entragues. Henceforth, instead of trembling before the word crime, he would have to qualify it. A preliminary distinction would have spared him the start which had frightened the dice players. Now he willingly accepted a Sixtine who was a neighbor to crime, and even a criminal Sixtine. In the latter case it meant, for example, that she loved, that she was deceived, that she had poisoned the deceiver. Ah! there are luckless poisoned ones whose fate may trouble sensibilities after the deed. But if, instead of defending herself, Sixtine had died, what sort of person would the assassin have been?

This crime, at first so disturbing, insensibly gained some considerations of attraction. An old desire, like an old viper, stirred in his head. Ah! to kiss hands that had used poison! To caress the flesh of a murderess! Through contempt of all morality, to give pleasure to the woman who had provoked, for her peace, frightful agonies!... And perhaps there truly was nothing in it at all! Oh! she had, with a single word, confessed too thoroughly not to go, some day, to the end of the avowal: he would know how to win her confidence. For the time being, as it was impossible to penetrate further, lacking sufficient enlightenment, Entragues abandoned all analysis and dined.

Afterwards, he recopied the sequence which, in his revery, had been dimly refashioned. The desired words took their assigned place, the rhythm polished the breaks that appeared too rude, the imperfections were effaced.

It went thus:

DREAM FIGURE

Séquence

La très chère aux yeux clairs apparaît sous la lune,
Sous la lune éphémère et mère des beaux rêves.
La lumière bleuie par les brumes cendrait
D'une poussière aérienne
Son front fleuri d'etoiles, et sa légère chevelure
Flottait dans l'air derrière ses pas légers:
La chimère dormait au fond de ses prunelles.
Sur la chair nue et frêle de son cou,
Les stellaires sourires d'un rosaire de perles
Etageaient les reflets de leurs pâle éclairs. Ses poignets
Avaient des bracelets tout pareils; et sa tête,
La couronne incrustée des sept pierres mystiques
Dont les flammes transpercent le coeur comme des glaives
Sous la lune éphémère et mère des beaux rêves.

He signed his name and the date, adding farther down, as an envoy "To Madame Sixtine Magne." To spare himself reflections of this sort: "Shall I send it to her, shall I not send it to her?" he addressed an envelope, affixed a stamp, and immediately carried it to the mailbox.

Then, to divert himself by gaining an hour of rest, he repeated the story with which Monsieur de B———. had amused them, one evening, at the home of the countess—a quite unadorned story, as becomes such a trifle—just such a thing as could be written by those whose occasional simplicity is not due to a poverty of language or to an imaginative sterility.

CHAPTER VII

MARCELLE AND MARCELINE

A story in the style of "Cinderella," but more modern.

"Ni vers, ni prose; points de grands mots,
point de brillans, point de rimes: un ton naïf
m'accomode mieux; en un mot, un récits sans
façon et comme on parle."
Madame d'Aulnay, *l'Adroite Princesse*.

Once upon a time there was a nobleman who took to himself a second wife who had as wicked a heart as you could imagine. They had a daughter who resembled her mother, and it was not long before the two were tyrants of the house, for this nobleman loved them and humored all their whims. Especially did the daughter take advantage of it to inflict a thousand miseries upon her step-sister, whose birthright seemed to her a theft of her rights as a spoiled child. One was called Marcelle and the other, Marceline. The wicked Marcelle hated her sister, but the good Marceline returned good for evil. And as her father, through very goodness of soul, and to have peace in the house, always took the part of Marcelle, Marceline learned to suffer.

Marcelle was as pretty as a bouquet of roses. Taught to smile by the smiles she had received at the cradle and while she played, she knew how to be radiant, and every one considered her a very amiable person. Tall and shapely, she had a white and delicate skin, red lips and long blond hair.

Marceline was ugly, small, with dark hair and complexion; in truth, she had very lively eyes, but they had a somber color and lacked any tender expression. She was mistaken for her sister's governess, and sometimes for her maid, for though no one was cruel enough to refuse her whatever dresses she desired, she affected a taste for simple clothes.

Marcelle had already refused more than one eligible suitor, when a young lord named Lélian moved her heart by his good manners, his title, that of a marquis, and his fortune.

The marriage day was fixed, Lélian courted in a most gallant fashion, and the only thing left was the arranging of the festivities that would signalize such a great way.

Marceline took great pains not to show any spite because the younger daughter was getting married first. On the contrary, she was as amiable as ever. With an unwonted good grace she welcomed the young marquis destined for her sister; this everybody appreciated and people began to find her less ugly and less displeasing. Marcelle, amid her joy, always kept the haughty air belonging to a well-born girl. Lélian felt more admiration than love for her and he was not displeased to talk a little with Marceline. The "little one," as she was contemptuously called, soon seemed to him more intelligent and pleasant than her sister. She spoke of all things with spirit, her good humor took no offense at any teasing, and when, by chance, she was alone with Lélian, a strange flame of an almost mysterious charm, shone in her somber eyes. By gazing at them long, Lélian discovered that her dark brown eyes had a perfectly nuanced gamut of expression: they were eloquent. From that time, and during the moments he was not paying court to Marcelle, he strove to spell out the words that lay in Marceline's eyes.

He thought of them as much as any man, on the eve of marriage, can think of eyes which do not belong to the woman he is about to wed, when Marceline, suddenly unwell, took to her room for three days. This was decisive: the dark eyes recovered their language so clearly that there was no mistaking them.

It was the very morning of the marriage day. Quite recovered, but still a trifle pale, Marceline strolled through the garden, touching the flowers without gathering a single one. Lélian, on his side, was walking about to conceal his impatience. They met.

What passed between them while they strolled, through the walks, silently and slowly? What did they say in the garden walks? Lélian, without astonishment, heard these words which Marceline, as she suddenly left him, threw like an arrow:

"And take care not to mistake the door this evening, for my sister and I have adjoining rooms!"

After the return from church, there was a great repast that continued far into the evening; then came dances and games in the illuminated rooms; then a magnificent supper was served, followed by more dances and games. The peasants, under a specially erected tent, took part in the rejoicings; they sang songs, discharged guns, danced, kissed one another, and drank to the bride's health.

While the ball was at its height, Marcelle disappeared without anyone taking notice, except the men among themselves and the women behind their fans; several young girls blushed; others thoughtfully followed the retreating train of white silk with their eyes. The bride's dress, her attitude, the least little word she had spoken in a quite distracted voice since the ceremony, her tears, her smiles, her kisses—all were passed in review. The old women, fearing ridicule, dissimulated the emotion brought up by distant memories; the young women sought the glances of their husbands in the throng.

Lélian mounted the stairs with a firm and rapid step. He saw the two adjacent doors. One was shut; the other was ajar. This one he pushed and entered. Without a sound, and with diabolic skill, Marceline turned the key and bolted the door.

Before the house was astir, Lélian led Marcelle away, as had been arranged. A coach, spanned and ready, awaited them.

After the honeymoon trip, which was brief, because of the quite natural impatience of the newly married couple to settle in their home, they dwelt in Lélian's château.

As the two domains touched each other, so to speak, Marcelle was able to find some happiness near her parents and her sister whom she had ceased to hate. Unhappiness softens certain prideful souls and Marcelle, who had promised herself many numberless joys, found herself, as happens, the most unfortunate woman in the world.

Taught by experience, Marceline refused to marry. When any one speaks to her of the miserable condition of an old maid, she smiles and asks:

"Come, are you so sure that I am an old maid?"

And it must be agreed that a sort of beauty flowered in the dark Marceline and that the white Marcelle grew almost ugly.

I believe that Marceline is a fairy, but this is not quite certain.

CHAPTER VIII

THE TRANSPARENT CURTAIN OF TIME

"In laying down his Cogito ergo sum as the
only certainty, and in considering the world's
existence as problematical, Descartes found
the essential departing point of all philosophy."
Schopenhauer: *The World as Idea*.

Entragues rose early and penholder in hand, turning over his papers while he drank tea and smoked cigarettes, he began the day.

Monsieur Dubois, through an administrative memorandum, had the goodness to inform him about his affairs. There had been postal supplications and telegraphic pardons. Madame du Boys was returning. The envelope contained the letter and the copy of the dispatch. Entragues appreciated this attention which would permit him to follow, without fatigue, the developments of the oratorio.

The letter, dated from Geneva, was a reply. The secretary, among indistinct phrases, had doubtless let fall the seed of hope, for Madame du Boys seemed to accept at the same time that she implored. Though standing on her dignity, she was not displeased with this rope flung in the midst of her muddled situation. She joyfully clutched it, with the naïve and vainglorious pleasure of being able to say: "It is he who is taking the first step! How anxious he is to have me! Ah! the poor man, I do not want to make him suffer any more." This could be read all around the pages, on all the margins, even on the envelope, which had been addressed with a poised hand. Too, there flowered a boredom from this international paper: "I enjoy myself more even in Paris, by the side of a stupid and solemn husband, than on the banks of Lake Geneva, where I am alone with my maid from nine in the morning till six at night—without counting the days when business delays *Monsieur le comte*—and where, to fall asleep, I drink, in the *Revue des Treize Cantons*, lymphatic emanations on the course of life and the meaning of death!"

"P. S. Say that I am passing a season in Switzerland for my health."

She arrives, lets fall her little bundles, opens her arms, and Monsieur Dubois, very agitated, falls into them.

"Ah! my poor friend, so I find you again! What trials!"

She has pardoned.

Monsieur Dubois dries his eyes, not knowing what to say; his flown discourse leaves him speechless.

Bending towards one of the little parcels which she lifts, Madame du Boys, serpentine and coy, murmurs:

"I have thought of you, dear one, I bring you a box of cigars."

Entragues was greatly amused by this unforseen denouement. He was just finishing the draught of a sketch when the bell rang; it was a letter with a handwriting unknown to him. The wording was brief:

"Monsieur d'Entragues is expected this evening to give a commentary on his *Dream*. Only auditors: the four walls and Sixtine Magne."

Two joyful tidings already, and it was not yet midday. It was only at this hour that his scanty correspondence was brought him, for the precious mornings could not be troubled by the intrusion of the external problematical world. Even amid a quite feverish contentment, he did not regret the instructions he had given once for all; Sixtine's letter came at a moment when he could think at leisure and without remorse. His pleasure was manifested by a vivacity of movement altogether juvenile; a semblance of adolescence surged from his precocious maturity. Though he generally was incapable of giving a clear account of his impressions, he felt himself rejuvenated, and this astonished him. He walked about with lively quick movements.

Rue Notre-Dame-des-Champs was almost gay.

A reddish brown made the sun-bathed Luxembourg, through which he strolled, resplendent. It was full of pretty children and flashing ribbons. Towards the Odéon he ceased to be aware of the things around him—a beaming cloud enveloped him. In the afternoon, having breakfasted, though he could not have stated how or where, he found himself on the Pont-Neuf, and collected his thoughts. Presence of mind returned to him and, dissipating with a last breath his cloud, he began consciously to revel in his happiness. The moment was brief: leaning on his elbows, looking at the unchanging water, he felt the premonitory thrill he so well knew; the frozen aura of spleen whistled in his ears and, bounding the horizon like a wall, the black Idea reared itself before him. An infinite distress overwhelmed him and, far from wishing the burden removed, he bent his shoulders, letting himself be crushed even to suicide. He closed his eyes with suffering, he trembled with cold, and a flicker of reason deep within him warned him of the absurdity of such a sudden and causeless grief. Yet he persisted, now lying under the avalanche of gloom, immobile, experiencing the garrot of solitary death, the slow excoriation of moral agony. This lasted an hour, during which he suffered weeks of real and profound pains, the cruelest pains ever invented by unjust human imagination, hopeless pains, infernal pains. He ached when he resumed his normal state and unsteadily went on his way.

The distraction of book hunting proved a great relief. The mummies, ranged in dozens in their tombs, awaited a momentary resurrection. He rescued several, *les Promenades* by Stendhal, which he did not possess, an old breviary embellished with armorial bearings, and a Venetian lexicon. He regretted having purchased the Stendhal. It was a subject of sadness and in the unhealthy state in which his crisis had left him, the mere material contact of these artless but bitter little notes might be dangerous. Bitter! For him alone, perhaps, for he found such desolation in it: "This Rome of the Popes, this womb of the ideal, this Ninevah of the purple, this Babylon of the cross, this Sodom of mysticism, this ark of sadistic dreams, this incunabulum of sacred follies, this generator of the new passion, this Rome, I never again shall see!" A tiny kingdom had openly stolen its traditional capital and the modern baseness had ratified the theft.

His sadness turned to anger. Entragues smiled at this quixotism, but the violence of even a fugitive indignation ended by making him sound again, and, recovering full consciousness, he breathed.

In the street, Entragues did not sympathize with the rumbling consciousness dispersed among the human fluid emanating from the throngs. The passersby seemed phantoms to him, he was not aware of them, considering them as inconsistent as the vignettes of an illustrated book. The most tragic public event only elicited from him an acquiescence or repulsion of the artist: to shrug the shoulders and cry: Bravo, Chance! A very scornful observer and thoroughly persuaded in advance that nothing new can be produced by the encounters of individuals with one another or against things, since the elaborating brains partake eternally of a fundamental identity and their visible differences are but the right and reverse sides of an untearable material embroidered with a durable and everlasting embroidery; conscious of the uselessness of leaving his house to enter another house which is just the same, Entragues loved the proximity of books that demonstrated to him the probability of his philosophy. He never tired of admiring the courageous perserverance of men who invariably repeated the same thing. All that had been written since the Bible could be resumed in three words; fired in a fantastic crucible, the totality of books would give this for a chemical residuum: cogito, ergo sum. Descartes was the only man who had ever expressed a necessary idea, and thirteen letters had sufficed for it. He would have wished to see them engraved on the front of monuments.

Outside of these three words, nothing indubitably existed except art; for it alone, endowed with the critical faculty, has the power of evoking life. It alone, without remarking the warp and woof, however, can variegate the embroidery of the stuff, because it embroiders safe from contingencies. The existence of Marie-Antoinette is problematical; that of Antigone is certain. The queen who died on the scaffold is at the mercy of deductions and negations; Antigone is as eternal as the family love she symbolizes, and the falling stars will not hush the piteous and charming confession of her feminine heart murmuring across the centuries: "I am born to love and not to hate." The symbol is as imperishable as the idea whose transcendental form it is and becomes necessary to it as soon as it clothes the idea. When you persecute Galileo, it is a man who suffers; when you separate Romeo from Juliette, it is the entire species that feels their anguish.

Having placed art above and even in the place of life, Entragues still doubted. Was art not an illusion as well? If the external world consists of phantoms only, could he create aught but phantoms, unless he confined himself to the eternal reproduction of the eternal ego? But at its highest degree of personality, individual consciousness contains all forms, and just as, by a necessary objectivity, it projects externally the silhouettes on the transparent curtain of time, which is life, it can project them outside of time, which is art.

The ant in distress swam boldly towards the last straw, withstanding the cruel waves; it did not founder in the hollows of the rivulet—which are for it larger than the ocean—and it saw safety when the motion of the waves raised it to the pinnacle.

His meditations were suddenly troubled, like the water of a pool into which a swan plunges. The jovial, merry instinct recovered its toy. There was now no means of arguing upon the illusion of suffering: the lashes of presentiment cut his back so keenly and severely that it was clear the hand could not be wheedled by any reasoning.

The child was amusing itself too well. "And yet! and yet!" All was vain and it was true. Entragues, upon returning to his quarters, found this mortal note, mortal in the state of exaltation in which he had lived since the morning, a damper that truly resembled death.

"Inpromptu dinner with the countess who has come on some business. Regrets. Let tomorrow take the place of to-day. S. M."

As he sat reading these lines, his head in his hands, without having removed his hat, gloves, overcoat and cane, he had the misfortune to wish to seek the secret causes; he passed, without stirring, two or three very painful hours. His reasoning went thus: in writing the first letter to me yesterday, she evidently knew how matters stood. He then asked himself why she was playing with him. He employed the whole evening in resolving this difficult question. Finally, after having followed several diverse solutions, he concluded: "Perhaps, as she said, it really was a simple accident." As aching as a victim of the inquisition, after his seance of torture, he fell asleep cursing hope, that torture more subtle than the wooden horse, needles and spiders, a sketch but lately illuminated by Villiers de l'Isle-Adam.

He fell asleep, living again the pages of the master in a terrifying nightmare, and only in the morning did rest come.

Upon arising, he was another person, and certitude, pure and clear certitude did not abandon him an instant until evening. At half past eight, the hour chosen and fixed by her, he would see her. Until then he walked with closed eyes, almost like a blind man, all the powers of his mind, all his faculties of idealisation, together with his scorn and skepticism, drowned in that drop of water—Sixtine. He did not even have enough strength for astonishment: a rising moon, a dawning love dominated his horizon. This unique contemplation, by gentle degrees, isolated him in a trance.

CHAPTER IX

THE PROMENADE OF SIN

"This curl of hair belongs to a daughter of
Ra-Hor-Xuti, who has in her every essence
of divinity."
Orbiney Papyrus, Pl. xi. 4.

A prisoner in her abbatial seat, she had quite the air of a fourteenth century person. Dressed in red, her feet rested on a black cushion; her fingers, lit with garnets and opals, perhaps with cassidony, and with agates, played with the white girdle which tied a robe with heavy purple undulations; her head, a pale flower, leaned against the carved wainscot; the shadow of the ogive framed the blonde aureole.

Altogether nonplussed by the attitude which seemed to demand the genuflexion of a worshiper, instead of the cordial greeting of a friend, he remained standing near the door, seeking some word to begin. For a few seconds Sixtine enjoyed the astonishment she had anticipated, then skilfully rose and, with a trace of lingering vanity, offered her hand. He took it coldly, seeing that she had tried to deceive him with a *mise en scène*.

The thread broke and all the pearls of the embroidery fell one after the other; it was the work of this evening to fill the silken thread, to put the scattered jewels back into their design.

Both busied themselves with good will over the task and Sixtine, who felt the peril of having travestied, even with a worthy attire, the primitive image remaining in the eyes of Entragues, quickly became again the simple and sincerely strange woman of the first hour. At least Hubert, at the sight of some gestures, at the sound of some words, so recreated her; he gradually recovered his ease and renewed with Sixtine the chat commenced in the country place.

The heavy branches of the firs drooped above their heads; a stag passed, hounds passed, Diana, on a golden crescent, passed.

Sixtine threw a veil of green silk over the rose-colored shade. She remarked:

"Diana provides her own light. The hunt will continue by moonlight. Is it dreamlike enough, thus?"

"It is in such a light that I beheld you one night, a surprising night of revery or vision: *E par chie sia una cosa venuta....*"

"*Da cielo in terro*," continued Sixtine. "My mother was Venetian; she made me read a few Italian poets. Some scraps of it have remained; she did not even give me her hair, for I am blond like my father, a pale blond that is my despair, for I have not a blond soul."

"Do you think that the soul and the hair are always of the same color, almost to the nuance? It is true that nuances are of consequence. The feminine hair assumes more than thirty tints that are entirely different and can be depicted by precise words, half of which are daily used, but at random. These tints blend and intermingle to infinity and the very eye can hardly define them by immediate comparison. This is so true that, as you know, you can never match hair. Would it not be amusing to make a classification of feminine characters according to the terms of the nuances of their hair? It would suffice to determine the exact tone so as to be able to pronounce upon the character, the passional faculties, the inclination towards friendship or love, the sentiment of duty, the maternal tenderness, and the like. Those *somnambulists* who make use of this principle without method and without preliminary studies, occasionally reach curious revelations. In five or six years, this science will be perfected, and those who possess it to perfection will be able to determine a man's character through a lock of hair, and will know what to do in order to take advantage of him. But fools and the ignorant always escape the power of intelligence; they will acquire the facile ruse of shaving their skulls, and this will once more prove the futility of all knowledge and the vanity of mind."

"Apply to me the science of to-morrow. What is the color of my soul?" asked Sixtine, wishing to make use, like all women, of the least general idea.

"A changing blond, a flame blond, or if you wish to decompose the nuance, tawny, ash and gold. Tawny is savagery, ash is nonchalance, gold is passion. Your horoscope will be like this: a woman fluctuating between the desire to be enchained to tenderness and her love of independence, but who will resign herself to the choice which circumstances make for her; as indolence is a bad body guard, it is probable that she will be won...."

"Taken!" cried Sixtine, "taken! I told you so. I await the robber!"

"Indeed, it amounts to the same thing. Won or taken by some one she perhaps will not love, but who will have been finer and stronger than the others. Conclusion: the final acquiescence of her nonchalance."

"No! not that. The robber must please me. But why the future? Perhaps the destinies are already accomplished? What do you know of that?"

"Oh! nothing," said Entragues, somewhat troubled. "Only, men always dream in a woman's presence of the morrow, never of the day before. It seems that the morrow belongs to them, as a necessary consequence of the present moment, and when they cannot regulate it for their personal profit, vanity, at least, will not be displeased to adapt it somewhat by insinuation. The most foolish among them believes himself born to be the director of conscience; and, in fact, since they cannot govern themselves, it is perhaps their true vocation."

"It is certain," Sixtine answered, "that women are not happier for having won the liberty of the bridle on their necks. They generally want too many things at one time to wish seriously for any one thing, and it is rendering them a service to fix the road where their desires can gallop more at ease. Unfortunately, tyranny is neighbor to good counsel; one cannot always distinguish one from the other. That is why we have revolted. Then it is a great temptation to a man to legislate upon all things, as soon as a woman has accepted some of his advice; orders follow, despotism commences, and insurrection is justified."

"You speak, Madame, like a statesman, and I am astonished that you are not somewhat of an Egeria!"

"I was and I wearied of the rôle. So your jest is not to the purpose. It is perhaps amusing to lead women, but not men. The Egeria they want holds in leash a tiny plump creature with drooping ears; Rops has designed it, and while I do not frequent the private museums, I have seen it. An Egeria by day, and it is always the same one, whose soul becomes visible to their spirituality under the most secret and revealing hair. It is there they go to seek the soul's color."

Sixtine had spoken with a juvenile warmth which discouraged Entragues. It was the indignation of a woman whose intelligence has been disdained and who, considering herself a political collaborator, has seen her rôle reduced to that of a carnal instrument. He pretended to have only remarked the lively side of her talk, and replied:

"I did not dare, in my theory of the science of hair, to put all the possible harmonies in line. The clothes, moreover, make a further research altogether puerile, partaking of a sickly curiosity. Yet, though the agreement of tones is far from being perfect always, one must take account of it. Confess, too, Madame, that if it is not the palace and residence of Psyche, it is at least her country house."

"Well," said Sixtine, laughing good-naturedly, "I pardon you for that last word, but do not begin again."

"But it was you...."

"That is not the same thing. I did not insist. Hush! you will spoil for me all the verses in which tresses are mentioned, and even those of Berenice will become suspect. You have seen me 'under the ephemeral moon.' I would like to know just when."

"Seen? Yes! I have particular faculties of vision and sometimes I evoked you near me by magic. The object I strongly think about is incorporated before my eyes in a visible form and often becomes palpable to the touch. I have felt presences of persons who were actually quite remote from me. And this does not at all astonish me, for regular sensation is only a true hallucination. For me, it is a matter of indifference whether it be true or false. I hardly worry about it."

"Then all women are at your mercy? If a woman you loved shunned your entreaties, would imagination ... would imagination suffice?"

"No, that would be the vilest of sins, the most sacrilegious, and the most useless. Of what avail is an unshared carnal pleasure? No, such acts as those are only too dismal. I am not the unchaste passerby of the poet, I do not delight in ridiculous, incomplete and dull profanations. No more am I a Jean-Jacques. The Most High has not favored me with a gift that would be fatal to the women of my time."

"Do you believe that these hallucinations would be so disagreeable to them? For when one wishes to please, one wishes to please in everything."

"There are feminine perversities," Entragues returned, "that are sufficiently frightful to content one with the metaphysics of pleasure. But I see beyond. Parallel dreams strive, at the same moment, towards the same end. Result: mutual possession at a distance. What a triumph for love! What a resource for separated lovers!"

"It is not for you to speak of our perversity, you who are endowed with such a perverse imagination."

She gasped a little for breath and fanned herself, oh! without fear, the feeble sex, and with a firm head.

A short silence followed.

This unusual costume which had first broken Entragues chain of sensation, now delighted him. He was thankful to Sixtine for not having appeared in a house robe of the latest style, for this would have swerved the talk to the vulgar stupidity of Parisian gossip or of a dialogue in modern comedy. A somewhat different intimacy with Sixtine seemed extremely desirable; a second and identical bifurcation led his sentiment, starting from curiosity, to desire.

"Introduce me to your history." He repeated to himself the first measure of the symphonic sonnet, and the very affright, in its recall, pursued the heels of the desire.

She reflectively watched him, not without little impatient movements of her fingers.

"She who would make him her slave, would doubtless make him wise."

"Yes, doubtless."

Sixtine pronounced these few words gravely, in a cordial manner.

Under the green of the old tapestry that hung from the ceiling and covered a whole side of the wall, in the still and cool room, a warmth of spring was diffused in golden waves; it was suddenly wafted from the vaporized intimacy.

Uttering the appropriate trifles, to which Entragues lightly replied, Sixtine rose, lit a blue flame under the copper kettle, opened a box of cigarettes, moved about in such an adorable setting that he smiled with joy to see her go and come, lavishing pretty movements and beautifully arched gestures.

She poured tea.

"Now recollect. You owe me my commentary. What is that vision in which I appeared with 'the brow studded with stars?'"

He told of the astonishing apparition, adding that there was a story which Monsieur de B———. knew.

Sixtine interrupted him and pronounced the already familiar words:

"If you wish, I shall tell you the story of the portrait chamber."

Entragues started and grew pale. This exceeded the bounds of probability. With a weak voice, he answered:

"I really would like to hear it."

Sixtine began:

HISTORY OF THE PORTRAIT CHAMBER

"It is a tragic and rather strange story...." She stopped, seeming to summon her memory. Then:

"No, I should indeed prefer not to tell you it."

"Oh! please," urged Entragues, like a child who opens two wide, curious eyes.

"No, sometime later, perhaps. If you had asked it down there, before those verses, before a coincidence which I guess and which disturbs me! I cannot just now. When you learn it, you will understand, and this very reticence will seem clear to you.... It is said that it has never lied.... Well, listen: 'The Château de Rabodange at one time was the hereditary domain....' It is too much for me.... Childishness? Don't say that!"

"But I said nothing. The emotion I see you in does not suggest such words to me. Let us forget the story...."

"Well," replied Sixtine, "try to guess it. You can. I give you permission. Perhaps you will tell it to me. Let us talk no more of it and please go. I get up early and I must sleep. You see that I treat you like a friend."

She had such a nervous air that Hubert asked for nothing better than to obey her, not wishing to spoil his evening by the blunder of a reserve which henceforth might be necessary before the woman who no longer seemed mistress of herself. It was the moment for retreat or the moment for a bold stroke. He pursued the first course, the second not having entered his mind. When it was a matter of other persons, or when he reflected at leisure on his own sentimental adventures, Entragues possessed a remarkable lucidity of mind; before the cause itself—the cause in person, throbbing and eloquent—he was confused, like a school-boy, and obeyed, unaware of his stupidity, those false insinuations of women who ask for a violet so as to get a rose. He therefore made ready to leave, saying:

"I would not wish to oppose such good habits."

"Is it not written," she responded in the same light tone, "'flee all occasions of sinning?'"

"And even Saint Bernard, in his *Meditations*, considers the contemplated sin as serious as the perpetrated one. Not to flee the occasion is to anticipate the offense and render it inexcusable. But I do not see how early rising specially agrees with this precept. On the contrary, it seems to me that the longer the day, the more numerous are the stones on the road. Then, can it be that you want to travel along the road of perfection?"

"I am anxious not to soil my life with any chance entanglement. Are not evil connections less to be feared from seven o'clock until noon, than from seven o'clock until midnight? The most elementary reasoning would easily demonstrate this, I fancy."

"Ah!" Hubert said, feeling the need of a mischievous air. "You know the hours when Sin promenades, and have you encountered Sin?"

"Often," Sixtine jestingly responded, "often and Her Highness always favors me with a smile. She is not proud and she willingly offers her hand; you can see that she loves men in a friendly rather than in a princely way; between them is an old familiarity. Daily she returned with joy to the legitimate bed fallen to her lot. By an astonishing multiplicity of faces, statures, gestures, voices, Sin courts women, clothing herself in the dreamed-of form, and that is why I would rather bring to an end my promenade before she commences hers. But, I pray you, please go. Yes, come occasionally, at the same hour. *A bientôt.*"

CHAPTER X

THE UNLEAVENED DOUGH

"......................"
Vauvenargues
"La beauté c'est la forme que l'amour
donne aux choses."
Ernest Hello.
"Flaubert, pas de sentiment.... S'il l'avait,
cela, il aurait tout."
Conversations de Villiers de l'Isle-Adam.

Smoking, strolling about, making paradoxes—there were a half dozen of them under the distracted presidency of Fortier, who was correcting proofs for his first number of the new series.

"Good day, Entragues. You received my note and you are bringing me some copy. Now that we come out every fortnight, I am going to be very hungry, I warn you."

"Did you ever see a review lack copy—a review which pays?" Hubert answered. "Print Constance. You owe it to your subscribers. 'Every woman would like to read this new study of youthful psychology. The originality of the thought, the pure relief of the style, together with the profound knowledge of all the mysteries of the feminine heart, make it an exquisite masterpiece of the analysis of passion. Please insert.'"

"He promised me a novel."

"With an alluring title," interrupted a voice.

Entragues turned his head. A young man, with a correct and cold air, was looking at him. Fortier introduced them to each other. He was a friend of the countess. They surely must have met at the Marigny Avenue home? Entragues acquiesced in this insinuation, thinking: Tomorrow, or the day after, my poor Fortier, the countess and *la Revue spéculative* will belong to Lucien Renaudeau.

"The title?"

"Alluring," repeated Renaudeau; "it is called: 'Pure as Fire.'"

"This florist of souls quite pleases me," said Jean Chrétien, in a slow and rich voice. "I am looking over, among his books, 'The Wisdom of the Nations.'

It is full of incontestable truths. One walks here in a friendly garden: all the aphorisms of Stendhal and Balzac frequently crop forth. But if we wish to start a seriously symbolistic review, it is necessary to tempt culture with less familiar animals."

Sylvestre entered with a cloudy air and Renaudeau instantly addressed him in a harsh tone:

"Now tell us who is that counterfeit of old George Sand who came here yesterday with your recommendation?"

"With a dog under each arm?"

"A black and a blond one. She offered us copy, patrons, loans, her experience, romantic souvenirs, the last boots of Alexander Dumas, cards of the chief of police, the address of a photographer and three copyists, an interview with Bouvier, the right to reprint the complete works of her late husband, tickets for the coming Elysée ball and for women, too, I think, but that was a bit vague."

"Oh!" Sylvestre gently answered, "she is old and poor, she must make a living."

"I do not see the necessity," Renaudeau said.

"A fine silhouette for a 'Parisian' novel," Fortier said.

"Doubtless, because it would be true?" asked Jean Chrétien, a poet who professed Buddhism. "Would you become a modernist?"

"A naturalist," said Fortier, laughing, "I want to make money."

"I fancy you will want to a little later," said Entragues. "The original cavern is empty. Do you take Huysmans for a naturalist? But his *A Rebours* is the most insolent mockery of this very school, when he simply replies to Zola's "*naturiste*" and democratic enthusiasm:

"Nature has had its day!"

"That is a book!"

"A disheartening book," Entragues continued, "one which has confessed in advance, and for long, our tastes and distastes."

"Yes," Chrétien agreed, "but I am speaking of others, of the naive souls who believe that because an object moves it must exist. Nature! but it is the artist who creates nature, and art is only the faculty of objectifying in an image the individual representation of the world.

"And," Passavant put in, "man himself is only the image of the idea."

"In that case," Chrétien answered, "far from attaining the absolute truth, as those ninnies boast of doing, art is but a reflected image—the image of an image. It is no longer the will which acts directly, but only a will already fixed in the individual, subjected to intelligence, weakened by division, in short, limited to whims."

"Such writers," Entragues remarked, "are, like the generality of men, almost the whole humanity, victims of an optical illusion. They imagine that the external world acts outside of them; this is a transcendental stupidity, but which is not necessarily produced by their special esthetics. The world is the idea I have of it, and the special modulations of my brain determine this idea. They have ugly brains, that is all. One could make amusing sketches in this way: the world as seen by a crab, the world as seen by a pig, the world as seen by a helminth. We describe ourselves, we can describe only that; an artist's creation is the slow and daily reaction of intelligence and will on a certain mass of individual cells."

"It would then be necessary," Renaudeau said, "to accept them as they are! Not quite. One can recreate oneself, cleanse one's low nature, take it to the Turkish bath, sponge it, rub it until the blood circulates. You are too indulgent, Monsieur Entragues."

"Entragues," said Calixte Heliot, who just then entered, "loves nothing but art and interests himself only in style."

"A novelty, indeed!" Entragues replied. "Unfortunately, art is not sufficient to produce style; a gift is necessary. Without that thing which Vauvenargues calls heart, Villiers sentiment, Hello love, literature is an unleavened dough. Look at Flaubert; he is a peremptory and sovereign artist who congenitally lacked love. Do you think that Villiers, by the most diligent labor, could have effaced from his work the stamp of his proud personality! Compare *Bouvard et Pécuchet* with the *Contes cruels*; there you have the patient genius and the spontaneous genius, resigned scorn and indignant scorn, a hurt intellect and a wounded soul...."

"Are you bringing me your poem, Heliot?" Fortier asked. "Just put it in the closet with the masterpieces."

"Thank you," Calixte said, simply, as he opened a huge portfolio.

From it he drew his manuscript, where could be read, on the first page, the author's name, Calixte Heliot, in a very beautiful flowing handwriting. He was proud of his Christian name. Then he brought out a small case and slowly untied its strings.

"Here is a masterpiece for you. Eh! What does Van Baël think of it?"

The art critic took the little yellow paper, a delicate etching, and pronounced:

"Good, very good, a little dark, too deeply bitten. From afar," and he stretched out his hand, "from afar it turns to aquatint."

"By whom is it? There is an S and an M interlaced at the left-hand corner."

"S M, S M," repeated Van Baël. "I cannot guess. It is a portrait. I see more letters after the monogram. Strange, strange ... It reads: S. M. to S. M. A laconic dedication of the author to himself, or else a strange coincidence of initials."

Nobody, not even Entragues who studied it intently, could find the key to the monogram.

Hubert and Calixte were old friends who owed each other valuable services. Calixte observed Hubert's insistance: a fatidical attraction, rather than curiosity, fascinated his eyes, keeping them glued to the engraving.

"You can have it if you wish, my dear Entragues."

"I accept it," Entragues replied, "but with the permission of being able to return it to you or else to throw it into the fire."

CHAPTER XI

DIAMOND DUST

"Chino la fronte e con lo sguardo a terra
L'amoroso Pensier rode se stesso."
Cav. Marino, *l'Adone*, VIII, 12.

More than two weeks had passed since the feverish and mysterious evening which Sixtine granted to Entragues. Three times he had tried to see her, three times he had failed: irritated, exasperated, cast down, such were his three successive states of mind.

After the door had closed on him, by the gleam of an instantaneous if tardy clairvoyance, he had seen and deciphered Sixtine's final irony: "You do not take me? Yet I am at your mercy. I have the air of thinking, of listening, of speaking, but I do not think, I do not listen, I do not speak—I merely pretend to do all these things and I await. Yet another half-hour, another ten minutes, five, one, the last one, nothing! Go! you make me lose my patience!"

"Now," Entragues told himself, "it is quite well reorganized, I must not lose it." And going by the longest route to his home, meditatively he recomposed the scene, wrote it in his mind. How Would it go at the theater? He planned the play. While the man in love explains the tenderness of his sentiments, the woman disrobes. He shrugged his shoulders: this would not be understood, he would be charged with coarseness. And yet the comic Plato had already done it, then Andronicus, then several Destouches, several Picards and several Augiers.

One could pass on a little note to the eminent professors who lecture on dramatic history (that vast science in three hundred thousand *feuilletons*): Note.—Cf.: *Plato com. Frag. ed. Brulend.* §3;—*Andron. ap. Taschend.* t. XXXVII; etc. In the matter of books, criticism buries you, in the matter of the theater, it overwhelms you. To write for one's sole pleasure, with an absolute disdain for present opinions. Yes, but if they are just, that is to say favorable, one glories in it. Isolation is difficult, vanity ceaselessly and indefatigably solders the cable one has cut. Vanity! Fatuity! And in everything. Thus this monologue lends itself to Sixtine. I reason like a male; and she feels like a female and I shall never know what she felt at a certain moment, because, even taking for granted a confession and the wish to be sincere, she would lie by nature. The truth is what one thinks it; when one no longer thinks of anything—all is reduced to nothing! There remains sensation, but analyzed sensation—diamond dust!

He went to bed feeling miserable, and as he was dozing off with the consciousness of his moral powerlessness he was seized with a fit of despondency comparable to that of impotent men when in the presence of the desired woman. Incapable of loving, incapable of tearing from his heart the parasitic science whose tentacles strangled him, it seemed to him as if he had swallowed plaster, as if muddy blood stagnated in his veins; or rather as if his arteries slowly carried a curare which gradually benumbed his muscles. His mind obstructed with the most contradictory metaphors, he tried them one after the other, vaguely disgusted with their absurdity. Finally, with a rush of vitality, he somewhat reconquered his logic and ceased to hold himself in contempt: "I suffer, hence I love!" This thought, though he ironically perceived its mild naïveté, comforted him, a very long and decisive breathing reëstablished the haematosis, and he was able to sleep peacefully.

Painful doubts of this sort came to torture him on more than one evening. He was only delivered from them by anger—the first time that he knocked at Sixtine's door without getting a response. Certain deceptions on certain days determined this action, when strong desire had a precise end. At this moment it was to see Sixtine, merely to see her, merely the pleasure of the eyes.

The effect was the same after the second check, but accentuated to a sort of rage, a hardly dangerous crisis whose very lashes were salutary.

The last mockery of fortune, on the other hand, threw him into a resigned dejection. "She does not want to see me; I have displeased her, but how? Yet I love her." Thus displaced from the subject to the object, doubt was supportable as an imposed pain which one accepts without having any responsibility: "It is not my fault."

So he paced the streets or visited his friends and the *Revue spéculative*, a pale melancholy upon him like the vegetation of a cave. Under the shadow of a strong habit which no disturbance could uproot, he still worked in the mornings, but he shortened the hours, impatient for his distracting strolls. His imagination no longer accompanied him. It seemed that in ever projecting his thought towards an external creature, he had proportionately diminished the intensity of his evocative faculty.

As he was leaving the *Revue*, after Fortier had told him that the countess, now installed in her home because of affairs, was receiving some friends on a certain evening, at nine o'clock, he discovered that the present day was Wednesday, the day in question.

"Perhaps I will find Sixtine there?"

This quite natural reflection guided his somnambulism towards Marigny Avenue. In the interval he had dressed and dined with a perfect unconsciousness. A system of newly organized revery relieved the slow and rude friction of transitions; furnished with a problem of metaphysics, commerce, art, politics, it mattered not what so long as it required shrewd deductions, he used to be so perfectly absorbed in them that the hours vainly pricked him with their pins, the minutes. He walked through the streets insentient, inexistent. But, involuntarily, this action of his mind which shut him in between the walls of the fixed idea was a grievous imprisonment against which his will rebelled; on the other hand, chosen and brought about in entire freedom, this incarceration saved him, without the tax of suffering, from the ennui of expectation. Nothing was so painful to him as changes of rhythm. He wished them to be abrupt or imperceptible, partaking of a sudden brutality or of an infinitesimal gentleness, the unity of force sustained with all its initial violence or decomposed into the infinity of its diminishing fractions. Leibnitz had taught him the arithmetical method of reducing the sensation of time to an evanescent progression: he applied the method to life. To live and not to be aware of living was an ideal to which his senses, deceivers, but unrelenting, too often barred the road. Today the obstacle had been surmounted.

In the small modern room on the ground floor there were many people: some raised their heads when his name was announced; the usual movements and whisperings:

"An Entragues?"

"Which Entragues?"

"Oh! some stray stem of an Entragues! The name is quite common in the South."

"Yet he carries himself well."

"The countess will tell us about him." As soon as he was freed from the ceremonial of introduction, Entragues sought the eyes of some friend with whom he could be at ease. He found Sixtine's eyes: a gesture beckoned him.

He obeyed without astonishment, for he had seen a chair near her, guarded by a fan.

"I noticed you. How criminal I consider myself towards your friendliness and insistence.... Do you want me to number your visiting cards? Why did you not write to me?"

"But I wanted to see you."

"Yes, but writing has a witchery unknown to printed forms. Instead of seeking me, you should have called me. And you have sought so badly!"

"No, since I find you at last."

"By chance! Are you satisfied? You wished to see me, well, look at me."

"That is what I am doing," Hubert responded, "and with pleasure. I would never grow tired of it, Madame."

"I supposed it was quite the other way," Sixtine rejoined, "and that a secret or very inconsiderate presentiment informed you of my absences. How one blames one's friends! For the past three weeks, I left three times, in the evening, to come here, and naturally on the Wednesday of each week. Admit that it was odd for me to find your card, each Wednesday that I returned home."

"I am lost if you suppose I did it purposely," Hubert answered, "for every explanation is too simple to seem probable. I will give you the best one, although it may not perhaps be the true one. The first evening in which I passed a few minutes at your home was a Wednesday. A latent force must have led me to your door on the following Wednesdays, and this without any participation of my will. This periodical return, like the regular culmination of a feverish condition, is after all quite natural."

"These are the reasonings," Sixtine replied, "of an automaton who would be hard put to explain why he always plays the same tune on the flute, at the same hour. But you have come to the countess, instead of knocking at my door. Did no one wind you up this morning? On whom does this task devolve?"

"It would be yours, Madame, if you consented."

Each of them, ill at ease, felt the same desire to be silent and to go away. Sixtine, not yet calmed after the old ill-humor that had finally exploded, feared to hurt Hubert, feared to bleed him with too many prickings. Hubert, who feigned a sad politeness, endured suffocating agony. So he had been judged and Sixtine had pronounced sentence, with what aggravations for the unhappy man! Incapable, perhaps, of loving; certainly incapable of sharing his love. Would no mirage, then, be able to deceive him persistently, with sufficient certitude to give him courage to lead across the desert, towards the oasis, a phantom of love vivified by desire? She scoffed him and he surrendered; she fled and he watched her flee.

At the foot of the stairs which she had rapidly descended, remorse seized Sixtine by the flap of her cloak; she turned her head and waited for several seconds. Then, lifting her skirts, she hurried to the carriage which a watchful gamin, upon noticing her at the sidewalk, had motioned with mock gestures of obsequiousness. Profiting by the new indecision, remorse tried to seduce her with these insinuations:

"The air is very pleasant, the sky is clear, it would be nice to return on foot, chatting on the way. This poor Hubert would appreciate it, and I have really been a bit severe with him: he asks so little! But what can he be doing?"

She listened: no sound of a person issuing from the house. "What is this! You seem to be waiting for him! What an attitude for a woman!" the thin and whispering voice of feminine vanity breathed to her. She gave the driver her address and climbed into the carriage.

Hubert had slowly walked down the stairs stopping at each step. He staggered under a fit of contempt. His whole person, the very necessary movement of his limbs seemed to him an insult to life. His reflection, perceived in the mirrors, gave him a horror of effectual futility. This careful attire—what a pretentious obedience to vanity I How ugly he was with his pale cheeks and empty gaze! Ah! dust compressed into a human form, what prevents thee from returning to thy natural state, where thou couldst humbly blend thyself, as would be fitting, with the bruised and scorned sand crying beneath thy phantom feet?

He reached the gate; a carriage, detaching itself from the file, departed: "Perhaps it was she? No, she must be far away, by now. The air is very pleasant, the sky clear, it would have been nice to return on foot, chatting. This pleasure was not made for me, and it is ridiculous even to dream of it. Yet, would she have refused me, if I had asked? Eh! there I reason as if this woman had the slightest liking for me. Shall I, then, never cure myself of the stupid presumption with which I so grievously delude myself? What is the good of my philosophy? Everything is useless. Ah! I suffer less! The futility of my life is not unique; it is confounded with the universal nothingness. Yes, but all the same I can only consider myself, only myself, since I know nothing outside of my consciousness. Well, then! I remain alone, indemnified and invulnerable. What is that cloud, called Sixtine, which comes to trouble my royal indifference and to conceal my sun—death? I do not want to go to sleep in the shadow of her beauty. What is the good of loving, when the awakening is certain. Ah! if eternity were given me! Indispensable eternity, without you life is only a quite despicable thoroughfare. Does the present hour exist for the condemned person who knows that the next hour will not belong to him? And this life is less than an hour for whomsoever knows the worth of what he has been deprived of in being robbed of eternity." How he would have sacrificed his genius to be a Christian and no longer a dilettante of Christianity, believing, not in the unique beauty, but in the truth of religion, assured not alone of his social necessity, but of his immutable, absolute and solar truth!

He issued from his metaphysical cloud near the Pont-Royal, and fell back into his actual misery. The woman he loved did not love him and would never love him. In vain he scorned himself, in vain he accused himself of emotional impotence, the man deep in him protested and repeated: "I must love, since I suffer."

But, with Entragues, the man never pronounced the final aphorism. After the troubled divagations of the lover came the romancer, an artist or ditch-digger who gathered impressions together, clothed them in words as with a shroud of chatoyant folds, and laid them to rest, with care, respect and tenderness, in the vault whose portal bears the words written in letters of gold: *LITERATURE*.

He went to sleep, dreaming of the embryo of a romance which a more disinterested person would find in this new adventure. But perhaps he would some day acquire that necessary disinterestedness! At first the idea was outrageous, then he grew accustomed to it; he mentally sketched a first chapter—that of the encounter. He transported the scene to Naples, at the end of the fifteenth century, and the personages became pure symbols. The Man, a prisoner, typified the idea of the soul imprisoned in the jail of the flesh, quite ignorant of the external world, refashioning the vague vision transmitted by the senses. The Woman, a madonna, was a statue which the prisoner's love endowed with life and feeling, becoming as really existent to him as a creature of God. And on this theme could be developed all the divagations of love, dream and madness.

On the morning of the next day, he commenced this story which was closely based upon his actual state of mind, and in which he would take delight in transposing, in a manner of logical extravagance, the drama he was naively playing with Sixtine.

This madonna was the new woman, *la Madonna Novella*, and what name should be given to the prisoner, a prey to his own imagination, if not that of *Della Preda*, since we are in Italy. *Veltro* fits the indispensable turnkey, and for title—*The Adorer*.

CHAPTER XII

THE ADORER

"*Ave rosa speciosa!*"
Innocent III.

I. Blood Red

Sainte Napolitaine aux mains pleines de feux,
Rose au coeur violet, fleur de sainte Gudule,
As-tu trouvé ta croix dans le désert des cieux?
Gérard de Nerval, *les Chimères*.

The night entered through the loophole—the end of a day of horror. He had been forgotten; he had not been given his daily walk. Perhaps he was going to perish here, without seeing the Novella again.

Morning, noon or evening, according to the arabesques of his fancy. Veltro, his jailor, opened the door with a violent turn of the key: "To the tower!" Delia Preda obediently climbed the few steps of the narrow and dim stairway; he climbed slowly, as if to perform a duty to which no exception could be taken, for he knew that these daily moments of apparent liberty in the open air were given to intensify the horrors of his cell and to prevent him from losing the notion of time and the duration of his torment. It is to reach this end rationally, without doubt, that the modern, rigid philanthropists instituted strict regulations in the new prisons. In 1489 the chief constables of Naples already knew the means of preventing these abuses of confidence by which the condemned person transmutes his punishment into an evil dream; but this was reserved for the prisoners of distinction. Guido della Preda, Count of Santa-Maria, was accused of having conspired, some said against the security of the State, others against the queen's honor. Because he was a gentleman, they had not hanged him; they had not beheaded him because he was innocent; a special punishment had fallen to his lot, for in a royal jail a difference must be established between prisoners who are guilty and those who are not.

He was in solitary confinement; the consciousness of the injustice he suffered might have led him into attempts at escape or revolt, and his intelligence would have made him the chief of the rascals sprawling all together on the straw of the common dungeon; and it is not fitting that a prisoner leave the prison through the window or that a jailer be strangled in a scuffle: it sets a very bad example and is liable to discredit prisons. There was yet another reason for this refinement, a privilege discussed and accorded by the State Council at the request of the Holy Office (for Della Preda was one of the thirteen peers of royalty): "Our Guido is innocent according to laws of this world, but who can boast of being so according to eternal laws? Let him, then, suffer in advance the punishment which God reserves for him upon his entry into the other life! Let him suffer more than the others, since he is less guilty! Let each hour of his mortal life be a painful preparatory measure leading to liberating death, through which eternity opens! Ah! What a good fortune for him to have been implicated in this action!"

The nineteenth hour sounded, seven o'clock according to our mode of reckoning time; by habit, Della Preda lifted his eyes towards the space framed by the high walls, and then towards the beginning of the arch, but he only beheld the night. This clock indicated the time for him by ringings violent as trumpets, and truly the pious desires of the Holy Office were being accomplished: the mortal hours of his mortal life fell one by one on his head, like leaden balls.

But all had not been foreseen! What holy monk could divine that within himself the prisoner would find joys and torments which not even the venomous Parthenope could have aroused in any heart.

The Tower of the Cross (*Torre della Croce*), so called at that time and for the past four hundred years the Tower of the Prey (*Torre della Preda*), dominates with its battlements all the vulgar quarters of Naples. It rears itself at the extreme end of a mass of old ruins still serving as a prison, through custom, and to which the people have given the name of Prison of the Blood-Hound (*Carcer delle Veltro*). At the end of the fifteenth century, these ruins, of a somewhat recent reconstruction, had the appearance of a fortress, and a space of a hundred and fifty feet was free between the walls, flanked by moats, and the first low houses of the outskirts.

At the center of the platform where Della Preda was daily led, a guard house was built which divided it in two, save for narrow passages, and limited the view on the side of the country. As he placed his foot on the last step, the prisoner had opposite him, to his left, the town which stood out in the distance, full of square belfries and domes; to the right was the blue gulf.

A church with flying buttresses, heavy and in ruins, first draws the unaccustomed glance and fixes it by the splendor of its brilliantly ornamented madonna. When the setting sun sank to the end of the pointed niche and bathed her with rays, the rubies and chrysolites of her tiara, the lepidolites and topazes of her starred aureola reflected the brilliance of luminaries and the faced adorned with diamond eyes looked rapturous.

The first time that Guido climbed to the tower was an evening when the sun was setting. He saw neither the flashing town with its green terraces, nor the blue bay with its white sails; but, uttering a cry, he asked:

"Down there! Down there! Who is that lady?"

"That lady? What lady?" repeated Veltro, with an astonished, already uneasy eye.

"Yes, that lady in front of the church of the Orphans?"

"Ah! you mean above the portal? That's the Novella, my lord," Veltro replied, baring his head as he pronounced the name, "a blessed and benevolent madonna. You can hardly see her well from below, the street is too narrow, but everybody knows that she is there, and that is enough."

"What an agreeable woman!" answered Guido. "O Novella! Protect me and love me!"

He knelt, bending his head, and when he stood up, after the last words of his supplicating *ave*, the *Novella* was smiling, full of grace and tenderness.

"So you accept my prayer? Thanks, madonna! Deign to receive me as your worshiper, let my breathing be a praise to your immaculate tenderness, to your sovereign grace. Open your goodness to the irrevocable gift of my life. Let me be to you as the pupil to the eye which moves it as it wills. Trample me with the blessed weight of the adorable feet which crushed the serpent! Let my flesh, for love of you, be withered, my bones broken, my blood shed. Ah! I love you, I Novella, blessed and benevolent madonna!"

The madonna accepted the pact: a sign denoted her wish, her choice and her pleasure. Three times her eyelids drooped over her eyes and three times they were raised. Then night fell and it seemed to Guido that a most notable miracle had suspended, for several instants, the sun at the horizon's edge.

"He is guilty, quite guilty," Veltro reflected, "but he has piety, he regrets his crimes. May the madonna listen to him!"

"Listen to me, my lord," added the jailor, "and know that there is no better recourse in the world than to implore the *Novella*. You see it is not for nothing that she is called the Madonna of the Orphans! Her arms always are open and she does not carry a babe because all God's creatures are her children. She is the only one, at least to my knowledge. *Santa Madonna degli Orfani, ora pro nobis.*"

During the two months that the Novella had been Guido's mistress, she had given him only happiness, charming and adorable happiness. He loved her and she smiled upon his love, except on certain days when a light cloud made ashen the pure face or the clear eyes of the beloved. He loved and, absorbed in his worship, felt himself loved. At first apprehensive, his tenderness now grew daring. The gentle but eternal smile no longer sufficed. The lover felt passion's boldness grow in his heart, like an imprisoned rose impelled by its sap to throw the living treasure of its purple to the broad day-light. The hour was approaching when the timid adorer would demand some tokens from the silent adored one, oh! the merest tokens of an adoration that was shared; the hour was approaching, the hour of communion, the spiritual hour which takes its sister by the hand, the hour of serious and tender eyes, the hour of strong caresses—the carnal hour.

The dark day which he passed under the hammer strokes of the pitiless clock was all the more painful to Guido since he had chosen it for definite questionings. Like all others, like lovers, he wished to know how matters stood, when it is simple to direct one's own questions and answers: but that is perhaps what he did, and why do anything else?

Veltro explained. It had been the fête of San Gaetano, the country his wife came from, about two leagues from Naples. He had received permission, had left, like a mad-cap, without informing the valet charged with his duties. "Would his lord the prisoner be good enough to forgive him?"

"Yes, Veltro, I pardon you. You are not bad and I believe you will not let it occur again, when I tell you that I have suffered greatly."

He slowly mounted, as to a certain joy, half shutting his eyes under the prolonged caresses of desire, counting the steps, trembling at the approach of the last and thirty-third.

A sudden alarm arrested his customary transport as he reached the battlements: he advanced hesitatingly, with gestures of astonishment and deception.

"Yet it is she, it is really she, and I do not recognize her."

"Set your mind at rest, my lord, there is nothing the matter, quite the contrary. They have put on her summer robe, that's all. The Novella changes her attire each season. And then there was a holiday, as well. Ah! if I had known! But how beautiful she is! She is beautiful as a queen."

Yes, she was beautiful. But Guido paused a moment before admitting this transmutation in which he had not at all participated. He sadly regarded the new Woman, sadly and with reproachful eyes:

"Are there seasons for my love? Are there days, are there hours? I loved the sky-colored robe which you had put on for our first meeting? Why then have you doffed it? Was it intended for me, at least? Did you wish to surprise me with a richer vesture that would more nobly become your serene beauty? Ah! queen, this too comely cloak does not bring my heart nearer to your heart, nor your lips to my lips; then, to what avail? You were blue like the sky and the sea, blue like the dream, blue like love—why this bleeding purple? In what stream of blood have you dipped your grace? Had I not offered you the torrent of my veins? Queen, you have betrayed me! You still smile at me, but your smile is cruel, you scoff, you scorn! An unfriendly day was that one in which, far from my tears, you permitted barbarous hands to profane the limbs I adore! It was I who should have divested you, it was I who should have covered you, divine and nude, in the sacred cloak of my effusions! Ah! you make me weep, Novella! What! you too weep, dear Passion, so you do yet love me? Oh! weep not! Pardon, pardon, I am the wicked one, I am the inclement one, and, moreover, I was mad. It is conceivable: I thought I had lost you. But no, it is not so? You are mine, more than ever, only mine! Let me be truly happy! No? Heed me, I love you! Not yet? It is true, I did doubt you; it is necessary to suffer, I wish to suffer."

CHAPTER XIII

CHRISTUS PATIENS

"Elle ne jugeait pas, ayant d'autres pensées."
Villiers de l'Isle-Adam, *Isis*.

"In this so lightly tilled field, where the corn has been so hurriedly sown," Entragues told himself, "I reap nothing but problems, tares, weeds, ridiculous rank grasses! For three days I have had only the worry of a mathematician intent upon insoluble x's."

SERIES OF X's.

xa.—It was poison.
xb.—History of the portrait chamber.
xc.—S. M. to S. M.

xa

"I believed I could find the solution. In truth, the problem was buried; it sprang up again, evoked by the two others."

xb

"Is it a history in which she is implicated? Is a page of her life written in this mysterious chamber where innocent travelers are favored with such astonishing visions? Must this second x be joined to the first one? A crime might have been committed there."

xc

"There is no doubting, if heaven has endowed me with some divining sense, that one of the mono-grams signifies Sixtine Magne and perhaps both resolved themselves into the identical syllables: a homage of the present to the pact, of the Sixtine of to-day to the Sixtine of yesterday: a portrait of the lover or husband, since she was married. Ah! I have it! Her husband had a Christian name commencing with S. It is a question of finding an engraver with the name of S—— Magne and that may easily be ascertained at some print dealer's shop; or else, in the case of a lover, S—— M——. Upon what do I base this deduction? On nothing. The twice-repeated initials of the woman I love ought to torment me, else I would not love her. Perhaps they only conceal names of no interest to me, but the 'perhaps' suffices to justify my uneasiness. The past? Enough of that. The present? Ah! the unknown enemy which one divines in smiles, in incomplete phrases, in gestures, and even in the little intimacies of the woman who lets herself be loved! A pleasant sensation and one which I still have not experienced! The jealousy without cause, the jealousy that nothing can cure—not even possession!... I must put down that remark, it is true."

He wrote several lines in his note-book: "Does a woman's supreme abandon prove her love? No, for this may be due to the occasion, to ennui, to the need of deceiving, to vengeance, to the perversity which throws her into your arms. To feel yourself loved, it is necessary to believe; love is a religion. You must have faith, you must love yourself. Love yourself? Yes, that is the means of being the more easily deceived. First to strip yourself of reason, then to plunge towards the truth! Absurd. Faith, then? Yes, to have faith, and is truth itself any thing except faith? Truth, faith—two aspects of one entity—the mystery of a God in two persons. Ah! if I believed that I was loved by Sixtine, she would love me, I would have peace, the joy of union. It can be done. How? Perhaps merely by not reflecting. To embark on the light skiff and go down with the current of water.... Towards the Ocean, yes, towards the ineluctable abyss? Evidently, but this detail is insignificant. The thing is to embark and not to pass your life in watching others depart for the exquisite unknown. But you return from it! Then what is the good? If the current is a circuit, it is just as well to remain at home and read the *Divine Comedy*. Alighieri himself returned! There is only death. But one never returns from death, and it is of little avail to another; but it has its answer ready and whispers it in the ear when it is so inclined. Bitter is life, more bitter is death."

A church stood near him. He recognized the humble *Saint-Médard*, entered and fell on his knees:

"O God of the Cross, Christus patiens, eternally suffering Christ, hearken to me! I seek joy, I seek love, I seek grief, and I find only a dreary void. I can neither enjoy myself, nor love, nor suffer. Take me by the hand and lead me as a mother leads her child. Must not one first suffer with thee? Then will come love, like rain in the desert, and joy will dawn, the joy of loving, the joy of having suffered...."

"I presume to pray," said Entragues to himself, lifting his head, "and I am giving vent to rhetoric. This prayer is welcome, and if I can remember it, I will use it. It would be blasphemous to take my note-book and write it down! Why not! One must profit from inspiration, for it can not be recovered."

He made a note of his ejaculation, with very slight variations.

"I stopped myself in time. The unconscious comedy would have made me blush in the end. Do I pray seriously and am I a Christian? Yes, I wish to be a Christian, and to partake of the most mystic and abstract Catholicism, when this would serve only to separate me from the abject mob, renouncing like a vile freedman the religion which drew it from slavery. It is quite evident that in my very heart I believe in the divinity of Jesus rather than in that of Sakya-Mouni and that I laugh at the vanity of an unconscious creator!...

"Ah! how enervating are these solitary rounds!"

Then, suddenly:

"I must see her, I must see her! Ah! provided it isn't Wednesday?"

The newspapers spread on the stand of a little bookshop told him that today was Friday, October 27. So ten days had already passed, ten irrevocable days since that dismal Wednesday when his love had collapsed. Collapsed! well, it could be rebuilt. But it really was too much, literally, to love at a distance. Sixtine did not, like himself, occupy her hours in analyzing everything and nothing: to have oneself loved, one must be seen. Henceforth, he would seek every occasion, he would follow her like a hunter, pressing her pitilessly to the very quarry of kisses. He would cease reflecting, and would think only of the end, counting obstacles as naught. He would commence from this evening.

His feet, already, obeyed, following this mental activity. He quickly ascended a popular street full of children, little democratic dauphins, brats of the modern sovereign. At this moment the inventor of popular suffrage seemed to him the most execrable monster produced by humanity and Nero and Attila, recast in a single model, compared to this unknown dastard, were creatures worthy of the genuflection. No one had abased the Idea to this point, no one had tried to make of the world such a desolate stable, where the kicking, respected Houyhnhms would have the ascendancy. He was a Pharisee and did himself justice for never having eaten the bitter hay of this royal rack: at the age of reason he had renounced, with disgust, his part in the sovereignty and never had a ballot soil his aristocratic fingers. This was due less to his early education than to subsequent and personal reflections, for modern degeneration accepts accomplished facts, and all that is left are single, inward and useless protests.

As he descended the Boulevard Saint-Michel, his step fell into an idle rhythm with the pace of the strollers. He looked around him and judged that no superior essence emanated from this other environment: here was the same evaporation of unconsciousness. Below, just as alongside and above, by devious ways people sought happiness, without suspecting, according to Pastor Manders, that it is open rebellion to seek happiness in this life. The social right was another political illusion equally chimerical. On this subject Herbert decided to read some Hobbes, at the first opportunity.

But did he himself, for example, consider himself above or only on a level with humanity? Ah! there is the intimate thought of each of the noble copies of baked clay which a God formerly modeled on the shores of the Tigris: I and the others, I and men, I and the rest, etc. It is thanks to this process that one judges, that one writes the novel or the story, that one rails in comedies or in shorter pleasantries. Judging is the universal and the particular, it is everything, it is life. Is not the famous tribunal, the tribunal of consciousness, with egoism for presiding judge and vices for assessors? And Hubert judged too: in defiance of all reason, he weighed the imponderable and fathomed the impenetrable, that is to say, the thoughts of others, without reflecting that one can know nothing outside of oneself and that to judge men, in short, is to judge the idea we have of men. Like the first of these prisoners, he had let himself be caught in the snare of reality: scoffing at those who sought happiness, he scoffed at himself, for what had he done since his birth in this world of sensibility except to consume the best part of his force in this quest? Vain and vainer than ever now that he was straying towards the external clouds. To what did he pretend, in loving Sixtine, and the yielding clouds dispersed, would he enjoy himself just as well with the fundamental night? When he broke the dear head between two stones, would he see what was within? One can doubtless use more human means and, for example, inoffensive fascination.

He returned to his preceding revery and the circle was closed; decidedly he must not reflect, he must act.

He found himself in excellent humor and quite ready, this time, to count without boredom the quarter hours on the clocks of the streets. He would even have willingly laughed with some chance companion, or considered the toddling of women, or strolled past diverting pictures. The Louvre, which he perceived from the other side of the stream, tempted him: he went to see once more the striking Clytemnestra so drolly illuminated with a torch and he was soon amusing himself in this room which, in previous days, he would have called a corner of shame. It did not equal, for comic intensity, the terrible Hogarths and the distressing Daumiers, but David and his school, nevertheless, had ridiculed antiquity successfully. The sober Flaxman had never succeeded in delineating personages so completely stupefied at having been cut out by a punch.

Entragues had once said that to make place for this foreign exhibition the paintings of the masters of an immoral nudity had been hidden in closets: it was the secret cabinet of the guards of the People's paintings. There remained to determine if bad paintings has not its own immorality and if the *Serment des Horaces* should not be put under key as well as the *Atalante et Méléagre*, the Parrhasius, perhaps a little exciting, in which Tiberius delighted?

From the arbitrary stupidity of the Neo-Romans Entragues went to the powdered heads of those enemies of the Nation and Humanity which David had designed, finally stripped of their paint, but so scornful that, one might say, he had lowered their eyes. The Pierrot gallery was charming and made you understand the Revolution, the envy of the People and its hate for graces so high and remote.

While leaving, and under the portices of the rue de Rivoli, he began to follow a woman whose restless gait, from the Cour du Louvre, excited his curiosity. She was not at all bad; she wore a rather original dress with black lace that fell in waves; but nothing striking. A brown pigment covered her eyes and served as a background, but there was no magical attraction: she was somewhat tall, slender, dark, very pale and the two sides of her face seemed unequal, because of the unequal droop of the corners of her mouth, the unequal lifting of her brows above heavy eye-lashes, one quite distended, the other in little contracted waves.

Nothing of caricature, but the sustained impression was painful.

The flat basket of an orange seller, at the corner of the rue de Marengo, and the sundry encumbrances of boxes and little wagons under the three arcades, seemed to exasperate her; she hastened forward, brushed against the fourth pillar, then against the fifth, then against the others, but sedately now, like a person who walks unconcernedly. If a group of persons collected around a pillar, she waited, brushed against it, and left; if the distraction of shop-windows had drawn her towards the other side of the walk, she quickly returned, as if with remorse at having passed one of the steps of her sorrowful path. Strict obedience to her impulse did not present her from noticing the curiosity of the passerby, but she had acquired such a skill, through long practice doubtless, such a deceptive gait, that no one noticed her.

She crossed the Palais-Royal Square, gained the Avenue de l'Opéra, all the time touching the gas lamps, trees and columns. There, she recommenced her maneuver with this variation: she touched each shop-door with her knee. One of them was opened; she waited, as before a precipice, gazing at the curtains of red plush of a milliner of ill-repute; she had such an unfortunate air that Entragues, with a discreet bow, accosted her:

"You seem troubled, Madame, can I be of any service?"

She looked at him, and not observing anything unpleasant in his tone or gestures, replied:

"Yes, you can save me, if you have any magnetism. Call a carriage, get in with me and take me back. I live at the Avenue de Clichy and am going there on foot without being able ... without being able to do otherwise.... You have seen me? As soon as I go out by myself, I walk, I walk ... and when I return, I faint with fatigue and shame."

Entragues had already, with his lifted cane, signaled a coachman, who drew near the pavement.

"You are merely a little nervous and need rest. Come, here is the carriage."

He took her arm; she resisted, saying, for the abyss had closed:

"Always this, nothing but this, the last one!"

She had set off again, turning her head supplicatingly, but without will-power.

"Well!" Entragues thought, "if I use force, the passerby will be attracted. As for magnetism, I can't see myself making passes at four o'clock in the afternoon, here in the Avenue de l'Opéra. It requires a severe glance and a commanding voice. What an odd adventure and what a queer hysterical person!"

Nevertheless he went and overtook her.

"Come," he roughly said, "the carriage is waiting. Come."

She lifted her eyes and, under his steady gaze, let herself be led.

Once in the carriage, she grew amiable, very amiable in fact; she told him secrets, spoke of her husband, of her little girl, her only child who was so dark and pretty, so capricious and wilful, breaking the heads of her dolls to punish them, throwing live coal on rugs to smell the burning odor, only liking salads, oranges and raw carrots, and not yet eight years old!

"Stop the carriage there," she said as they arrived at Clichy Square. "I am so grateful to you and you must come to see me. Would you like to be my doctor? Be my doctor. I will obey you implicitly."

"But...."

"You are no doctor, but what does it matter? So long as my husband believes it. He leaves at ten o'clock each morning. He is a stupid, functionary.... Ah! I am not understood!"

Her eyes, lit like embers, betokened an approaching danger. Entragues, who was concerned with quite other matters than the consoling of hysterical women, stopped the carriage, got out and said:

"*A bientôt.* I understand you."

She smiled, with a quick toss of her head. The carriage departed.

"She is at a crisis," mused Entragues. "Some one else will profit by it, for she is not ugly and should have, at certain moments, a sort of Maenad beauty. But I love Sixtine and feel incapable of loving other women. But why is it that so many women whom you pay no heed to, throw themselves at you, while the only one you desire shuns you?"

CHAPTER XIV

THE FAUN

"Sancte pater, sic transit gloria mundi."
Le Pontifical romain.

No sooner was he in Sixtine's presence than Hubert felt his pleasure spoiled by the questionings which an algebraic schema had laid down but had not solved. So his will to act weakened under the weight of the present. First he must decipher the puzzle.

He coldly advanced, with a calm smile, kissing the hand she gave him; this contact quieted his need of knowledge. Then, he asked himself whether the interlaced foliage of two or three problems would not form the necessary aureola around this fair head.

"And when I should reach the precise explanations, would I have added more beauty to this body full of beauties? As for the soul, I know that it is a secret coffer to which no one—not even she herself—has the key. And what could I do with it, and what could she do with it? So my anxiety is quite futile. What if I took her merely with plausible words, as the bird-call, by its mechanical song, captures the free birds?"

They spoke of different things, particularly of the falling leaves, and Hubert skilfully led, under the same stimulus, his revery and the conversation.

A Ziem, at the end of the room, cleverly illuminated by hidden lights, a resplendent Italian road-stead, with purple-tinted sails, many colored clouds in the sky, and over all a deep transparency, a sense of great distance, a brilliancy of atmosphere full of the magic of unfailing blue:

"Naples, a Naples I have never seen! Ah! that is because I scarcely look towards the gulf, for the Novella is my heaven and my ocean."

"Monsieur d'Entragues, why have you such a distracted air?"

This brought him back to the truth: he was not Della Preda, she had just pronounced his correct name, and Naples disappeared; after a few minute's absence, he found himself in Paris again, near Madame Sixtine Magne and before a quite good view of Venice.

"It is that picture," continued Sixtine. "It pleases me, but do not observe it too closely, for you will be forced to admit that it is mediocre, but charged with some power of illusion for imaginative minds."

While cursory words were being exchanged about painters and their paintings, there reawakened in Hubert, without any determinable cause, one of the most significant impressions of his adolescence. Feeling the impossibility of evading it and fearing a fit of abstractions, he repeated it aloud. The word "madonna" uttered by Sixtine furnished the pretext:

"Summer and a stormy evening. I had been restless all day; sudden languors made me prostrate; my nerves vibrated like harp-strings with each clap of thunder. My grandmother's harp rested in a corner of the room and when any one touched a door, it echoed. I compared myself to this mysterious instrument which I had once seen out of its rose silk case. I listened to the interior murmurings of my overexcited life, sounds welled within me, made me ill, and slowly went to a death of which it seemed I should die. Then the fears, the sweet fears of seeing, among the branches, a strange woman who would smile to me. Then the indiscreet titillations of pubescence which passed, played, breathed like a warm wind upon my skin. It was vacation time in the country: they had left me to my own devices and I rolled on the grass and ate it; I cut switches and shoots and instantly abandoned them; I climbed up trees and, half way, let myself slip with lax muscles. Obscene, vaguely understood couplets returned to me. Alexis and Corydon preoccupied me and I fancied that for the first time I understood the dim ardors of the poets. My desires were altogether formless. I had still another anguish: what was this malady which gripped me? Life would not be endurable, if I had to live thus. The night quieted me somewhat. As I annoyed everybody, that is to say my great-aunt Sophie, Aunt Azélia, an old maid, and the two house cats, dear and precious creatures, I was given pictures to look at, with instructions not to stir. They belonged to different parts of books given to quiet noisy children. Suddenly, as I was reading, I stopped, having found my childish ideal: the Madonna de Masolino da Panicale. Later in life I came upon that name under a quite different lithograph, alas! although it represented the same picture and the same madonna. I felt myself grow pale with emotion and confusion. The half-opened eyes gazed on me tenderly and the inflection of the head was so coy and amorous that my heart pounded. But the eyes soon preoccupied me above all the rest: I made a rampart of one of the leaves, I pretended to read attentively, I was alone with the divine eyes and gazed upon them. An hour perhaps had passed in this way but it seemed that I had hardly looked at them when the inflexible Azélia uttered the daily phrase: 'The curfew has rung.' Nothing rang in the house with its very old-fashioned clocks; so it was a metaphor; she always repeated it and I usually did not even smile at its mention. That evening I flew into a passion and I bantered the old maid so much that she sent me to bed 'without a candle, as cats go to the loft.' I fell asleep and slept as one sleeps at thirteen, but, in the night, the eyes of the Madonna visited me and I have since felt an inexplicable pleasure when gazing upon eyes that resemble the eyes of the Madonna de Masolino da Panicale."

As he finished, Entragues perceived that Sixtine had them, the very eyes; he knelt down and said:

"That is why I love you, Sixtine, and why I shall always love you!"

"Please, rise and let go my hands!"

"Let me keep them, let me love you. Ah! you are not indifferent, it is not possible."

"But," returned Sixtine, "I am surprised.... You tell me a very curious and interesting anecdote to which I listen without distrust, and it ends with a declaration.... It is very unexpected ... Come, sit down and let us talk peacefully.... I do not wish to discourage you, and I really want to be sincere.... If I loved you I would say so, it would even be a fitting occasion.... Frankly, I have not felt that little emotion, that tiny nothing.... Then how say it, I am very inexperienced ... It perhaps will come another time. Come, you will recommence and it will merely be a deferred pleasure.... I am quite willing to love.... My soul yearns for something.... It may be won, but you must conquer it.... How? That is your affair.... And then, you know that if I loved it would be for eternity.... There can be no casualness where such bonds are concerned. It is necessary to know each other, to estimate each other, to tell something of one's past life, to fathom characters, to analyze tastes. We are not children.... All this...."

"Ah! I am a fool," Sixtine was saying to herself during the pauses of her speech. "But I do not withdraw my hand, I only seem to ... So stirred, I would not wish to admit how delicious it has been.... No, it is an avowal.... Unexpected? I was waiting for it and would have been pained and surprised had it not come.... He is there, at my knees, at my knees: Oh! remain thus.... If I were he I should speak quite differently, but I like these doubts, these supplications. He is going to implore me again, again, again.... Do I love him? I am able to love him, at least I am not far from it, I feel that a certain word, a certain gesture ... and I would be in his arms, but will he say the word? Will he make the gesture?... Oh! yes! I have experienced something undefinable.... Yes, but I am not at such a point of ignorance.... Can all this be recovered, such moments?... Believe me, it is true, true, true, I want to love.... Well, take it, but be sure to take it. The word is too hard. My God, perhaps I am discouraging him. So much the worse, it will be the test.... Oh! to be fixed, to be bound forever! To him? I do not know, but if he wished it!... He is quite proper, but a little cold, and then, I already know him; he is capable of a profound sentiment.... What! he is rising, he abandons my hand, he goes to sit down on that chair, so far, so far from me.... Well, it is finished, and I am deceived. Let us wait."

"I believe I was wrong," replied Entragues, "to let you speak so long. You have recovered possession of your natural calm and now you are unattainable."

"I also think so," said Sixtine, wounded by this clumsy reply. "But I can assure you that I do not lose my head so easily. I have resisted more dangerous assaults and my virtue came out of them all untouched. If you expected to conquer me by surprise, you deceived yourself. Very strong muscles might succeed, perhaps, but the conquest would be quite precarious."

"You are mistaken, Madame, I love you too sincerely to count on the occasion and a mere physical possession, gained through the strength of one or the lassitude of the other. This is not at all my purpose. I wished only to obtain an avowal in return for an avowal...."

"There are mute women," Sixtine interrupted.

Entragues did not pursue the matter further. He contemplated the magnificent eyes which anxiously watched him, and he wondered how he could make them tender, how make them speak, for eyes speak without knowing that they do so, and are not masters of their language, like lips. Finally he answered, with the bitterness of deception:

"It is necessary to lose one's head."

"It is necessary, it is necessary: that is easily said. If he who proffers this aphorism first lost his head, it would be a different matter. Be indulgent to a very banal allusion: Whoever wishes to make others weep must be the first to weep."

"There are rebels and the spirit of contradiction makes great ravages in proud souls."

"I confess to a little pride. Without it there would be no dignity, but am I moved by the spirit of contradiction? I do not think so. If it were given you to penetrate into my inmost recesses, you would see, on the other hand, an infinitely malleable soul, a soul without definite form—a lump of clay which awaits the divine shaper; a woman's soul, in fine. But men judge women as inferior men; just as men, to women, generally are other women armed with superior strength. In truth, they are two beings as distinct as a dog and a cat, and it is always their unhappy fate not to understand one another, just like a dog and cat. What a distressing fatality, for one only exists through the other. Are they, perhaps, truly complete beings only in the fleeting moment when they are joined together? But it should be the labor of civilization and intelligence to perpetuate that moment by spiritual bonds, strong and supple ties whose physical meetings would be the consolidating knots. No, there is nothing more than actual desire and when that has fled, unassuaged, and one is well-bred, one has recourse to irony."

"It is a consolation," Entragues replied, "but I am refused it. I have never had enough presence of mind to juggle with my chagrin and divert myself by letting my eye follow the play of glass balls. Is my nature, perhaps, excessively complicated? Sincerity, like a diamond, has more than one facet...."

"Then," Sixtine interrupted, "it is a decomposed sincerity. Labor is needed to assist it to the state of pure light and all this psychological physics is too difficult a maneuver for my simplicity. If you only knew how simple I am, how simple all women are, dreadfully simple, my friend! In truth, one has but to take them by the hand!"

"Like the woman of a little while ago," Entragues thought. "Those whom one supposes strange are only more feminine women, thrust by their nerves to the extreme of feminity. It is true: to dominate the others, one must study them specially. Did not Ribot find the laws of memory and will in mental pathology? It would be excellent to make analogous studies of hysteria, but if the matter does not attempt it, who is capable of doing it? After all, the very subjects of the experiment have today given me two valuable lessons. Unfortunately, it is to be feared that they will avail me little in practical life. I am in a mood to live and I do not know how. Come, I will provoke her a little and guide myself by her replies. Women may be simple, but they appear artful and we can only act in their presence according to received impressions. Simple as a deciphered dispatch, simple when you have the key. What was she saying to me? I must answer. She is looking at me. Those beautiful large eyes! Ah! I truly love her!"

"Have me!" he exclaimed, falling on his knees. "I love you, I can say no more."

Her restless studded fingers clasped her knees that were covered with a red robe. Hubert embraced the knees and kissed the fingers. It was the same as happens with little serpents in skins of old silver found under withered ferns, in the sunlight; as soon as one touches them, they stiffen and become as brittle as glass. Sixtine, at this brusque contact, grew rigid as a lady of stone in her emblazoned seat, and Hubert felt that the least insistence would shatter that soul. It was too late. As Sixtine had so well conjectured, the startled occasion had fled. The very woman who, an instant before,—something Hubert did not suspect—would have surrendered for the present and for eternity to the first kiss, this same woman resented a new attempt at intimacy as an attempt at violation.

He obeyed and rose, but this time with more anger than embarrassment, for physical desire held him in its iron grip. Its nostrils held tight by a subduing apparatus, the bull occasionally resists under the stress of its anguish, routs its tormentor and rears itself, ready for vain accomplishments.

Before leaving, restraining his brutal unchained forces by a violent effort of will, he endeavored to reassure Sixtine by a playful amiability. Without returning to sow foolish explanations along the path he had traveled and which a wall, suddenly up-sprung, had confined, he smoothly indulged in metaphors and generalities upon love, made a dusky poetry gleam, paused at the scintillations of lyrical enthusiasm and succeeded in making the young uneasy woman smile, amused and perhaps moved by his good will.

He really felt that this evening had been somewhat unfortunate, but despair did not touch him. In short, nothing is irreparable. Then, too, he had acted and he believed that this was a great point.

CHAPTER XV

THE CARNAL HOUR

"And a thousand others, who never knew
what it was to have a soul...; yet, sir,
these men adorned society."
Poe: *Bon-Bon*.

Once in the street, Hubert saw the ardent eyes of an invisible spectre glaring at him through the gloom—two terrible, imperious and inciting eyes. He recognized them and an oppressiveness crushed him. They were the eyes of Lust.

"For women, the prowling phantom is called Sin—it is a male; for men it is the female Lust. Ah! yes, I recognize her. She is a companion of childhood. She is ingenious, She used to strum ballads to the moon on my adolescent nerves. Today, she drums the roundelay of the Lupanars on the back of my neck. With one stroke she wishes to degrade the lover and the love. I will betake myself to vile titillations and she whom I love will be the cause."

He reflected: a voluptuous dream brought on, from earliest adolescence, by the contemplation of the madonna's eyes; since that time, the association had been constant, often inexorable: he had to obey or suffer absolute insomnia, or else race like a noctambulist towards a retreating prey. In the last case, the winning talks at street corners little by little dissolved desire in the slow fire of disgust. But how terrible these nights when the shame of his obscene vagabondage overwhelmed him with horror!

Yet he did not want to go and knock, like an obsessed bourgeois, like clerks on paydays, at the latticed door of some sordid house, leading his idealism to promiscuous divans and submitting his body to the least withered bidder! He hesitated between a quite proper harem nearby, and the semblances of soothing intrigue: he did not despise a reciprocal choice that had the appearance of being voluntary, the excuse of a desire that fixed on this one rather than on the other, public preliminaries which are cleansed of all shame by the complicity of the environment—the Bal Bullier, for example, or the Folies-Bergère. By making a rapid decision and calling a carriage, he could reach one of those slave markets before closing time. Upon reflection, he abandoned the Bullier: the jades of this place were enjoying a rest. As for the other exhibition, it was quite far away.

Undecided, he grew composed. For a moment he hoped to have freed himself cheaply, but the eyes, the implacable eyes reappeared—obscene stars that would cease and vanish only at the clandestine house.

It was in a little street near the Saint-Sulpice market.

There, lived a woman whose eyes, adequate for his youthful dreams, had formerly captivated him—formerly, when he was about twenty—and no reasoned disgust dulled the senses. Each time his carnal obsessions evoked this pleasant memory he believed, with an animal waywardness, that he would find the same woman and the same contentment.

Since she did not surrender to the first importunate caller, having the coquetry of a certain amorous fastidiousness, one often found her either alone or able, under the pretext of a jealous protector, to turn out the guest of the evening, if the newcomer pleased her more.

"So this," reflected Entragues, "is the end? Honest women know quite well to what promiscuities they are exposed by their refusals; they should yield for the sake of dignity, at least. They should be taught this: it would be one of the useful chapters in the courses of love which old women could teach so well! But if they should yield, then farewell to the pleasant duels of vanity."

Without suspecting how futile and mischievous his reflections were, he followed the star.

"Now then, what is going to happen? Oh! I know in advance. None the less, I am going in!"

He knocked in a certain way.

"To think that I remember all this! Yet it is long since I came here. I have been spared these sudden and irremissible tortures for years. Years! She must be changed, old and ugly. All the better, it will be the necessary douche, and perhaps in a half-hour I shall be laughing at myself instead of crying. Perhaps she will be absent, or asleep, or engaged. Engaged! Like a school boy, I have a mind to run away before the door opens. One, two ... I am going to leave."

No, he knocked a second time.

"Who is it?"

"........"

"Toi!"

"She addresses me so familiarly, it is frightful."

"........"

"Yours forever!"

"Again! After all, I please her. It is less vile than indifference."

Now, whisperings reached him, interrupted by the opening and closing of doors. He had the sensation of conversations of nuns coming through a wooden partition. This sordid place had the mysteries of a convent; the approach of women and their movements always give man similar impressions, different though the surroundings be. She was debating with somebody; at last the bolt was unfastened, the key turned: another wait, but shorter, in a dark antechamber: the sounds of a second outside door, of steps descending the stairs: he had left.

She was dressed, a hat on her head, and gloved.

"Anyway, she has not just come from some one else's arms."

She had not aged. She was a warmly-blown summer which the breath of mutual happy moments had not withered. Women can withstand anything; neither vigils, nor fastings, nor repeated surrenders blight them; quite the contrary, in order to bloom, they cannot have too much care.

She showed her joy in little exclamations and tiny unruly words; Entragues thought it just as well to seize the present hour and attempt an amiable libertinism.

She thought him handsome and made for kisses; he let her go on, rather content with this impression and conscious of giving this woman, who was superior to her companions, a moment of sincere pleasure.

"These women, after all," he thought, "are not so repulsive as the adulterous ones; they lack, it is true, the aureole of deceit, but they are neither more nor less guilty: what is the difference between having two men at the same time, and having ten? With the second, vice commences; and if the latter must be scorned, the same scorn should be meted out to the former. Doubtless, since they are transgressing a stricter law and breaking a definitive vow, the adulteresses should enjoy a keener abandon, for hell-fire is already present in their kisses, if they have been favored with a Christian education; but how many of them are capable of so exquisite an enjoyment, of savoring in love the irremediable damnation incurred for the pleasure of him they love? One must grant them another possible superiority—that is, if there are children—for while the offspring of the unmarried have no father, adulterous offspring have two, a wise precaution against orphan-hood."

Meanwhile, Valentine had brought cakes and a bottle of that Aumalian wine which gives people the illusion of a princely treat. Then she grew tender towards Entragues, her eyes beamed forth cajolery, allurement, and promises.

She watched him dip his lips into the glass and wanted to drink after him, seemingly intoxicated with desire and genuine love, consoling herself in one evening, with this unexpected pilgrim, for some years perhaps, of exactions in which she took no pleasure.

A blasphemous comparison had made him liken her to a Magdalene suddenly seized with adoration, her soul just surrendered to a revealed God, lovely with inner and useless supplications, so persuaded to love above herself that a gesture of acquiescence would overwhelm her with joy.

This quite surprising spectacle charmed Entragues, but he felt his fault aggravated by this prolonged titillation. It had ceased to be the simple shock necessary to re-establish his composure, and had inexcusably become a pleasure in itself.

She kissed his hand prettily, the last traces of remorse fled—their emotions became identical.

They talked of trifles and he, employing those bagatelles which please women, made her laugh: she seemed, at times, astonished at her own delight, as if the cold air around her had suddenly and magically evaporated in effervescent perfumes.

The weak and ravaged Entragues seemed beautiful to her: blond hair, thinner and whiter at the temples, beard becoming a brown at the cheeks and ending in two long points as in old Venetian portraits; the brow high, the skin very pale but rosy in moments of animation, a curveless nose, a heavy mouth, eyelashes and eyebrows almost black over eyes gilded like certain feline eyes, but gentle. He had ordinary muscles and frame, carried his head erect, and seemed to be gazing at mirages, his eyes at once distant and steady, as if in a trance.

Valentine chiefly watched his lips. He perceived the fact and gave them. She was neither powdered nor painted, but her authentic self.

Entragues gazed at her with pleasure but without agitation, for the nude, especially in a woman's chamber, is not particularly sensuous; it is such a natural state, so simple, so free of provocation, so little suggestive by its absence of mystery, that a foot glimpsed in the street, a bodice cleverly arranged, a rustling of petticoats, an ungloved hand, a smile behind a fan, a certain air, a certain gesture, a certain glance, even with a wholly chaste intention, are much more rousing. A quite banal observation, but Entragues, pardonable in pausing to note it as a directly experienced impression, still sought to fathom its cause.

Now, he experienced a great discouragement: "I shall not have this beauty which pleases me, which I desire and which is mine. I can take her in my arms, I can press her against me, but I cannot have her. When I kiss her with as many kisses as deceit has tongues, still I shall not have her. And all the kinds of possession I can dream of are vain; even were I able to surround her like a wave, I should still not have her. The impulsion of love is unreal and it is only the illusion of desire which makes me believe in its possible accomplishment. I know it is error, I know that disillusion awaits me. I shall be punished by a frightful disappointment for having sought self-oblivion outside of myself, for having betrayed idealism, and yet it is unavoidable, for the senses are imperative and I have not merited the supernatural gift of grace."

Entragues had a prompter disillusion than he would have desired.

The adorable woman surrendered to his kisses; the carnal dream made them unconscious of good and evil; they advanced, eagerly and with swimming heads, ready to place their feet on the bark that sails towards the Isle of Delights, seeking to ascertain how the sails were shifting and the condition of the rudder. Entragues suddenly got up, pale; ghostly behind the window curtains, terrible in her red robe, Sixtine had revealed herself.

"Ah!" he vaguely thought, terrified, but his own self again, "this is reality. The illusions are reaped, the hay is brought in, the field is bare. This had to happen. The images which one voluntarily evokes come to acquire mischievous habits and evoke themselves independently. This one is impatient. So much the worse tor her; I did not invite her."

The bed curtains had to be closed and the lights put out. Sixtine spared them by not moving and by disdaining the stratagem of phosphorescence.

The candles, when after a while they were lit again, showed Entragues an empty room: Sixtine had departed. But departed also where the desires and all the unacknowledged pleasure of a delightful night of debauchery.

He dared not go out, fearing a solitude that might be peopled against his will. To fatigue the body is to fatigue the intelligence: he had enfeebled himself as a person stupefies himself with laudanum.

CHAPTER XVI

THE IDEAL BEES

"Afin de réduire le Ternaire, par le moyen du Quaternaire, à la simplicité de l'unité."
Le R. P. Esprit Sabathier,
l'Ombre idéale de la sagesse universelle.

"Ah! yes," mused Hubert, as he replaced the book in the corner restricted to philosophers, "the pages of Ribot's positive and disenchanting psychology make good reading at a moment, not of spleen, but of stark boredom. This penetrating dialectician clearly proves to me that my personality is a fragile chord which a single false note in the keyboard can destroy. It is all the same to me: a madness caused by a fixed idea must greatly assist in supporting life. Thus, collectors are to be envied, those who gather and classify old copper buttons, or old secret locks, or all that has been written against women, or the figurines of Sèvres porcelain, or the articles of M. Lemaître, or the slippers of historic balls. One need not be fastidious in choosing a mania: to be good it has only to be inexhaustible. As for the more distinguished follies, many excellent ones can be noted and, in general, none of those which are termed mild manias should be scorned: the people once knew this well, for they respected, in the persons of fools, the state of mind never attained by men of sense: happiness."

He continued thus for a long time, stretched back on his armchair, smoking cigarettes, wearied from his night and still enfeebled by a protracted bath. At bottom, he was deeply ashamed of himself, as after every similar defilement, and not at all reassured as to the metaphysical consequences of this sin. No reasoning, brutal though his unbelief might be, could efface such an impression. The being endowed with human intelligence and will always regulates himself by some rule, a mental guide that is often unconscious, but whose existence is immediately and with certitude revealed by the transgression. There is no common moral conscience outside of a religion that is strict and observed in all its commandments, the laws of society, and the special regulations belonging to a certain group: morality is a personal talent. Thus, Entragues felt himself soiled by an immersion in pleasure where others would still have enjoyed, even repletion, the gratification of a ruminant.

Moreover, he was not impious: having seen remorse rear its head before him, now that the hour of the bravado had passed, he trembled at the memory of the reproachful phantom. That night cut a phase of his life in two, and he saw himself equal to those whom physical existence confines beneath its claws: brother of the first comer and thrown back among the vulgar elements, he ceased to be himself. Ah! he had judged! Now he could be judged.

In this state of mind, nothing could interest him; since the principle of all interest vanished. Opium-like dreams benumbed him and all the texts on the vanity of things which he had gathered here and there in his readings, played under his skull, like the bell of a rattle.

Love, strangled by his hand, barred his path: to advance, it was necessary to leap over the dead thing: no! he would remain on this side, unless a miraculous and quite questionable resurrection occurred.

Glory! the bell has been melted so that little bells could be made. And as for the brass of the bells, does one ever know the right of the metal to the claim? One dies and the cracked sounds make the bell-ringers laugh.

He recited the proud and yet disheartening verses of old Dante:

La mondaine rumeur n'est rien qu'un souffle
De vent qui vient d'ici, qui vient de là,
Et, changeant d'aire, change aussi de nom.

Having put these three lines in French syllables, Hubert observed how difficult it was to clothe Dante in a fitting foreign garb. He pardoned the well-intentioned persons who had attempted it in scandalous translations: one could do no better than to adopt an exact, if disfiguring, metaphor: the precision of the original becomes loose, its clearness shadowy, for it is necessary to employ certain short words whose true sense is lost, and others which are no longer read except in glossaries. Finally, he laid down this aphorism: it is impossible to translate into an old and refined language a work belonging to the youth of a kindred language.

These technical notations, the reading of some verse, trips from his table to his library, had somewhat revived him. Although he felt that the depression might last all day and doubtless many more days, he recovered courage and believed himself fit for some light work. Hubert was not a poet, no more than many others who pretend to the poetic gift. His impressions translated themselves into little notes of analytical prose, not into fixed and exact rhythms; but he had learned the craft, knew the most modern secrets of versification, and in happy hours could, without illusion, fabricate an interesting piece according to the rules.

This morning, he succeeded in giving the final details to a diptych whose appearance had heretofore not satisfied him. It was heavy and the hammer beat had shaped it, directed by a hand that was more strong than adroit, but it seemed to him that the metal was good and without cracks.

MORITURA

Dans la serre torride, une plante exotique
Penchante, résignée: éclos hors de saison
Deux boutons fléchissaient, l'air grave et mystique;
La sève n'était plus pour elle qu'un poison.

Et je sentais pourtant de la fleur accablée
S'évaporer l'effluve âcre d'un parfum lourd,
Mes artères battaient, ma poitrine troublée
Haletait, mon regard se voilait, j'étais sourd

Dans la chambre, autre fleur, une femme très pale,
Les mains lasses, la tête appuyée aux coussins:
Elle s'abandonnait: un insensible râle
Soulevait tristement la langueur de ses seins.

Mais ses cheveux tombant en innombrables boucles
Ondulaient sinueux comme un large flot noir
Et ses grands yeux brillaient du feu des escarboucles
Comme un double fanal dans la brume du soir.

Les cheveux m'envoyaient des odeurs énervantes,
Pareilles à l'éther qu'aspire un patient,
Je perdais peu à peu de mes forces vivantes
Et les yeux transperçaient mon coeur inconscient.

The afternoon vanished, a very calm night conquered, he found himself astonished at the sudden return of vigor and of capacity for work. Three days after, he had completed "Peacock Plumes" and "The Twenty-Eighth of December;" he reread them, not without suffering from a sense of inmost shame, for although the conception of this last study was anterior to the luckless night, he had not been able, so identically did the situations present themselves, to develop his old idea except by borrowing from his recent adventure.

It had often happened to him that his revery intervened in the active series and broke its determination; such a result, certainly, no longer filled him with childish astonishments, but this time there was a truly marvelous subordination of the fact to the idea. This was the theme: faithless to a beloved Dead, A desires another woman, who yields and gives herself to him; but, at the moment of possession, the beloved Dead woman appears to him, in certain conditions to be developed, and the old love vanquishes the new. This outline, with some linear modifications, could symbolically have characterized the unexpected events of his night with Valentine. Presentiment and coincidence did not explain such an occurrence and, moreover, such an occurrence was the hundredth he had observed. Hence the conception of a possible event had brought it into his life, conditioned by the intervention of an external will, adapted to the vital limits of time and space, but recognizable in its constituent and original elements. It was worth reflecting upon: it was a whole corner of the yet unknown psychology, a whole order of phenomena as curious, for example, as the fact of suggestion so bungled by official hypnotizers, who lack philosophic understanding. This could even be classed under the chapter of suggestions; but if, in things of this kind, one knew the suggester, the person to whom a thing was suggested would escape. Nor was it a matter of a will dimly or even unconsciously domineered by another will; there was rather, as a point of departure, a will seeking to bring about the wholly ideal and wholly subjective accomplishment of a thing. But how could this will act upon the immutable order of things? Since the suggester found himself, in the case of the person subject to his will, in the second state, was it not merely a case of auto-suggestion? Then, too, it was necessary to explain how the subjected person could bring over, into his orb, wills and facts external to himself and how, in sustaining an order suggested by his mental activity, he could make it submit to all its relationships of things and beings. Idealism unveiled these dim arcana for him. Assuredly the thinking person dominates those who do not think, and the man who wills, though unwittingly, the realization, though ideal, of a group of facts, dominates all wills which, unwarned, are not on guard, finding themselves unprepared to oppose will with will. The material and unconscious world lives and moves only in the intelligence which perceives and recreates it anew according to personal forms; there is as much of the thinking world as a superior intelligence unites and fashions to his wish. The conflict is only among superiorities, and the rest, the herd, follows the masters, willy-nilly: ah! revolt is quite useless.

Entragues consequently found himself arrived at that point of intellectuality where one commences to make himself obeyed: order, apparently incoercible, yielded to his dream. It was now a question of mastering the dream and will. This was quite different: never having cultivated that faculty, he only possessed it to a rudimentary degree. The method was clear, he should have known how to make use of it; he could not and the world, without a doubt, would escape him. His regret was moderate: his desires did not exceed potentiality. The ideal world, as he held it, sufficed for his activity which was entirely mental and too unarmed for the struggle.

He had chosen the best part: should he be mad enough to consent to a disastrous exchange? Everything belonged to him in the sphere where he revolved: under logic's eye, he was the absolute master of a transcendent reality whose joyous domination did not give him leisure for a vulgar life and human preoccupations. To will? To will what? Ah! how much more interesting it is to watch oneself think: what spectacle equals that of the human brain, that marvelous hive where the ideal bees, in their nest of cells, distil thought: a fleeting activity, but which at least gives the illusion of duration. Ah! merely illusion, for only the eternal exists.

At this point in his revery Entragues was bitten by a serpent: the external, disdained and almost disowned world was evoked in the image of Sixtine. It was necessary to admit it: he had interests in this part of the perceptible world.

Then returned the same lamentations: fear, hope, doubt: love, composed of these three terms, ever arose, leading the trinity to unity and it was a circle, imperious as a circle. He lived a whole day in this prison, then towards evening a quite sharp sensation of indignity struck his heart and this obsession, poisoned by the arrow, inflamed the wound: "I am going to see Sixtine, I want to see her, but if she yields to my entreaty, the idea that she surprised me with another woman will make me fancy that only jealousy inclines her to unshared desires, and I will be paralyzed. I should do better to return to my home." But the image was stronger: he obeyed the suggestion.

"Ah!" he told himself, always capable of strict reasoning, "I am afraid I looked at the work of the ideal bees from too near a view, I well know that I think, but I no longer know what I think."

CHAPTER XVII

THE ADORER

II. Peacock Plumes

"Aria Serena, guand'apar l'albore
E bianca neve scender senza vento ...
Ció passa la beltate ...
De la mia donna ...
... Non po' 'maginare
Ch'om d'esto monde l'ardisca amirare ...
Ed i' s'i' la sguardasse, ne morira."
Guido Cavalcanti.

It rained peacock plumes,
Pan, pan, pan,
The multicolored door glowed with flames.

The sky of the bed trembled towards an oarystis,
It rained peacock plumes,
Plumes of a white peacock.

The tower waved gracefully like a felucca undulating in the evening sea breeze. And it was truly raining peacock plumes: Guido was astonished and blew at them. He caught one in flight: it was white, with an orange eye and luminous spaces. Ah! they all seemed to be looking at him: they paused in front of him, they smiled, they fell, they died. As they neared the earth, the wind spun them around a little, some dust floated, then they disappeared; the passersby did not even raise their heads.

The tower leaned over until it touched the ground: Guido leaped into the street. He was not deceived. The peacock plumes had disappeared: from below they could no longer be seen. It was a pity, for they were pretty. He continued to walk in full liberty, his head high, full of joy, watching the women. He passed under the madonna without emotion, threw a glance towards the portal of the church, which he found as ugly as a wagoner's gate, and of the Novella he only saw a madonna in trappings, wholly devoid of attractions. Nevertheless he bowed to her.

The door was gay with oriental robes: a negro in white was ordering some women into a curtained carriage; the women were caged like the Carmelites of Saint-Augustine when they go to get food. One was in blue, one in red, one in green, one in violet, and one in yellow. The first four climbed into the carriage, laughing like children and uttering rapid strange words. Guido, who had approached, saw that each one bore, pinned to her monkish cloak, a label behind her head. He deciphered the writing on the violet woman who was gesticulating a little less than the others: *All eccellentissimo e nobilissimo signor Ricardo Caraccioli*. So they had a certain destination! They were not to be let free in the country among the grass, the bluebottles, the poppies and crocuses? But what would the *seigneur* Caraccioli do with such flowerets? Guido knew him: he was a gentleman of exemplary habits, the son of a cardinal, and nephew of the late pope. What would he do with that young girl? A dialogue informed him:

"Are they all for the same most excellent *seigneur*?" asked a subordinate officer who held a large book in his hand.

"All for the same man," the negro answered, "at least they are all bound for the same name. Does it surprise you? But he will share them with his friends. His only fear is that they will seek to quarrel with him."

"Where are they from?"

"The devil only knows! We captured them off Algiers. A fine galley, all gilded, with flowers, feathers and perfumes. The captain towed it to Palerma, where he was able to dispose of it at a good price: that's his privilege. These women were on it; three old women and eleven men, a pasha, his equipage, keepers. No time was wasted: the men were thrown, bound and bleeding, into the sea. What a crew of bandits, eh? Eleven less and the old women thrown into the bargain."

"Five Turkish women," the other returned. "That's fifty ducats for the king and a flask of wine for me...."

"Good, let us drink."

"... In women," continued the *doganiere*, "and in specie."

The negro paid. They drank at a nearby tavern, their eyes never straying from their merchandise.

Guido understood that they were slaves destined for the harem of the most illustrious Caraccioli. At Venice, where he had lived, it was customary, since the Turks were pirating, to return the compliment. If this was becoming popular in Naples, so much the better; he would gather, into a little house, some Oriental women for his pleasure. Guido was neither sufficiently naive nor spiteful to believe that the most excellent hypocrite was carrying on the trade of fair eyes for his friends. Well! he could do likewise: arm a vessel, dispatch it on long cruises to the Barbary coasts, nourish the enlisted bandits with salty provisions and the captive beauties with blancmange.... Ah! he suddenly remembered: all his wealth had been confiscated by the crown! Not even a ducat in his hose; not a sword, not a pistol to procure money on the highway, and bareheaded as a Lazarite!

He would have to attend to this penury.

The office of the royal customs-house was opened and the overseer was drinking to the fiscal ransom of the Algerian women: he entered. The arrant employees of His Majesty were drowsing pen in hand, of course. He pushed another door, though perceived: a third one, and the treasure. From a very fine collection of garments, hose, cloaks, swords, pistols and French hats, he provided himself with a quite gallant outfit, added a remarkable piece of Alençon silk, a little string for the women, and some rope for the silent strangulation of the cashier. It was a small matter to pass through the three doors where pleasant dreams were stirring, and he found him a little farther away. His sleep was hardly broken: a little movement of the hands, nothing more. Without being very rich, the royal coffer was still interesting. He placed it in his pockets, untied the rope, returned it to its place, and strolled out.

On the threshold, the *doganiere* saluted him:

"Does Your Excellency deign to be pleased?"

"Yes, yes," Guido replied. "These gentlemen are polite. Here," he added, taking out a ducat, "go and drink with this."

The negro counted his women: one, two, three, four.... "All's well. No, I should have five. Let us count them: one, two, three, four, five."

The carriage departed.

"I love you, my lord, let us go!"

The yellow Algerian, appearing before him like a radiant caprice, had taken him by the hand.

"As soon as I saw you," she continued, "I hid myself so as not to be led away with the others, for I belong to you, I am your slave. My name is Pavona."

"But," asked Guido, "how were you able to see me with your closed eyes, for I know that, under your hood, your eyes are closed!"

"It is true," said Pavona. "You know me then?"

"Yes, I know you, you are she who was destined me to vanquish the Novella's disdain. When I beseeched her love, the consent of her passion, so many times confessed and yet never decisive, she closed her eyes, she said: 'No.' And I said: 'Well, I will love other eyes so that the eyes of the Novella might weep and be merciful to me.' Then her eyelashes lifted and I grew pale with fright: instead of the blue and gentle irises, I saw strange eyes like those designed on the plumes of a peacock, a white peacock."

"I do not understand anything of this," said Pavona. "I never open my eyes, for a very simple reason. I cannot. But I shall love you well all the same, you see!"

"You have never tried!"

"To open my eyes? No, and for what purpose, since I have none. Wait, I remember an oracle sung to me by the Bohemian woman, formerly, when I was very little. It had this refrain:

But when some one to you will say
'I love you!' sight will come your way."

Guido found this very natural.

They stopped at a rich tavern, dazzling as a palace, and they were received like princely persons.

Preceded by a servant, they climbed, climbed, climbed, as though to the sky.

"Carry me, Guido, or I will be quite tired," said Pavona.

Guido took her in his arms. They climbed, climbed, as though towards the sky.

"Kiss me, Guido, or I shall grow quite bored," said Pavona.

Guido kissed the closed eyelashes. They climbed, climbed, climbed, as though towards the sky.

"Here," said the servant at last, "is the apartment of Your Highnesses."

The multicolored door truly glowed with flames, for it was of silver and studded with diamonds.

"It is heaven's door," said Pavona. "I wish to open it myself."

She entered first, holding Guido by the hand.

There was a very agreeable blue dimness in the chamber: the couch, at the end, defined itself under heavy draperies.

Fondlings and caressings: Guido felt himself burn with desire, and Pavona, quite determined, returned his kisses, ardor for ardor.

"I love you," Guido cried.

Pavona opened her eyes.

They were fearful. They were like the eyes designed on the plumes of a peacock, a white peacock.

Guido swooned and awoke in his cell, an assassin, a thief, a perjurer.

"I am a wretch," he thought, after a moment, "a wretch unworthy of his own pity. The crimes one commits in dreaming, one is really capable of committing. What occurs in the dream lay dormant in the caves of the will, or rather, they are prophecies and the celestial admonition of an irrevocable predestination. Ah! rather to have been criminal than to live in the certitude of a future crime. I accept the weight of my mortal sins: by degrees penitence will dissolve them like a sack of salt by the rain, and my shoulders will straighten again, delivered. Pardon me, most holy madonna, and punish me."

Ah! l'amour est terrible et je souffre d'aimer!
Comment bénir encore tes adorables pieds?
Comment, d'un front souille par des lèvres de femme,
Recevoir le divin sourire où joue ton âme?
Comment bénir encore tes adorables pieds?

CHAPTER XVIII

A COMPLETE WOMAN

"Feminine to her inmost heart, and feminine
to her tender feet.
Very woman of very woman, nurse of ailing
body and mind."
Tennyson, *Locksley Hall
Sixty Years After*

He had a fair skin and a savage mustache, his beard cut like the Austrians, an animal jaw, beatified eyes; the air of needing plenty of meat and plenty of tenderness. His skull seemed to be straight, under his closely-cut hair and his ears, too long, seemed endowed with a special motility. His gestures revealed the uneasy deference of the stranger, but on occasion there appeared the sudden hauteur of the gentleman; he lacked an easy bearing, but there was some vivacity and a rude charm in him.

Hubert, examining this intruder, assumed a reserve which masked his curiosity. He thought he perceived that for Sixtine this was more than a chance visitor, and the name awakened a discouraging association of ideas, for it strictly agreed with the initials, although this person, it seemed to him, had no connection with the portrait, so far as the figure was concerned. His name was Sabas Moscowitch.

Sixtine spelled out the syllables with complacency and, after uttering a few banalities, narrated some pages of the history of Monsieur Sabas. A life not unlike Tolstoy's, without the final mysticism: a period of living in the Caucasus and then at his manor, in his domains which were disorganized by the recent freedom; he had a reformative turn of mind in sympathy with modern trends, and had won successes at the theatre with dramas of conflicts which had displeased the czar; then, and this was the interesting side of Monsieur Sabas, he had come to France to have his dramas played. As he knew French from childhood, he was translating them himself. Yet some advice would be profitable to him: he likewise had need of some support in the literary world. She boldly anticipated the kindness of Hubert.

"M. d'Entragues could be very useful to you."

Entragues, in a very guarded tone, offered his services. To read his dramas, present the author to the *Revue spéculative*, give the cue to Van Baël, who knew everybody, win over Fortier—all this was possible. Besides, Fortier was seeking new things: it would be a good idea, after the novels, to attempt the publication of a Russian drama. One of them would appear in the *Revue* with a great hubbub, and the road would be prepared for the others.

Sixtine seemed enchanted with the plan: Moscowitch had a vision of the glory he would gain; Entragues said to himself: "Either they are making a fool of me, and I have nothing to lose in being amiable to this Russian, or else she is only interesting herself in him through vanity, and the more I do, the more she will be grateful to me. No, I shall certainly be a dupe and without reward; there are old relations between them: the S. M. proves it. Oh! how anxious I am to mock gently before being mocked myself by the facts. That would mean to lose all. Ah! but I am implicated in odd intrigues! I must examine my acts carefully and weigh my words: it is painful. Ah! how I should like to leave! How I wish that I had never known this woman who holds me here and compares me with the other! I see it quite well: she is analyzing us, in so far as a woman is capable of doing it; she measures and weighs us; she asks herself which of the two would give her the greater pleasure. And perhaps she is embarrassed, for if one of us, and it is I, should attract her by the physical and intellectual affinities of race, the other has for her the magic of newness, of the unexpected, of the different. For she is perverted: without this, she would have a husband or a lover. Women who wait, who want to choose, who desire the utmost possible, are capable of deciding suddenly under the pressure of an unaccustomed sensation. But is it the first time she has seen this Moscowitch? Oh, no! but as long as the veil has not been lifted, the mystery remains untouched and still tempting. The exportation to France of Russian novels should be an enterprise for the Don Juans of the Neva: one must be, at this hour, a Russian to please. Oh! it is quite immaterial whether we shall be Russianized to-day or in a century, since we will be so, eventually: Tolstoy is the ensign-bearer and Dostoevsky the trumpet of the vanguard. *Amen!* I open the door to Moscowitch. If they play his dramas in place of mine and if he takes the woman I desire, well and good, for deprived of all, I shall perhaps enjoy peace."

Having finished this inward monologue, hardly interrupted by the nodding of the head and the vague syllables thrown by him as replies in the conversation, Entragues, with a sudden movement, arose.

"You are leaving?"

There was such an accent of reproach in these three words that Entragues was stricken with remorse. It was a foolish act: he soon saw its consequence, for Moscowitch instantly stood up to his full height, ready to follow him.

"Since it is too late, and since the pleasure of a tête-à-tête eludes me, we will leave together. I wouldn't mind talking a little with this Russian and, if he must be my rival, learning his quality; at least I shall know to whom I yield my place."

He was a child.

"Isn't she truly charming and adorable?"

"Ah! confidences?" Entragues told himself. "This is excellent. He belongs to those whose heart overflows with sentiment as a brook under a heavy rain, and he is going to tell me his life. Perfect. I am conscious of a mischievous curiosity. How I will enjoy it!"

A slight quiver of joy coursed through him, and his fingers twisted through nervousness.

"Isn't she?"

"Are you speaking of Madame Magne? I have known her only a short while. She is an intelligent woman."

"It is evident," Moscowitch rejoined, "that her beauty, her charm, and her grace have not made a strong impression on you. It is surprising."

"Why so? The sympathies of any group do not necessarily go to the same woman, though she have intelligence and an Aspasian beauty. The charm that has captivated you does not exist for me, or exists only in a less degree."

"Ah! you reason like a very sensible Frenchman. As for myself, I believe I am incapable of reasoning on this point."

"This does not prevent me," Entragues returned, "from doing justice to her qualities. She is, to put it simply, a complete woman. This word, which implies everything and specifies nothing, is appropriate, for I believe her to be very flexible, and made to pattern herself, like the ivy, on the oak to which she will cling."

"I hope," Entragues reflected, "that I speak clearly and with an abundance of commonplaces, for I wish to be understood."

After a brief silence, Moscowitch slowly uttered these words which he seemed to be repeating to himself:

"Yes, I think I will be happy with her."

Entragues controlled his emotions and asked in a calm voice:

"Are you going to marry her?"

"Yes, if she consents. That is my intention and my dearest wish. She says neither no nor yes. I don't know what to do about it."

"You don't displease her?"

"You think not?"

"I mean," Entragues answered, "that you please her. But she herself does not know it and you must teach her to read her own heart. Recall the words of Madame Récamier to Benjamin Constant: 'Dare, my friend, dare!' You perhaps don't know the French women, but trust to my experience. A little force doesn't displease them. I don't say violence, I say force. The iron hand gloved in velvet can play a decisive rôle in love; nothing more enlightens a woman about her own sentiments than a kiss which goes further than kisses. Then she knows what she wishes and nine times out of ten she will love, through gratitude, the bold man who has drawn her from indecision. Note this well: she runs after her modesty as one runs after one's gold."

Moscowitch, very interested, drew nearer to Entragues and, as if to appropriate him to himself, passed his arm under Entragues', saying:

"May I?"

"The great liberty? Ah! you know your authors! I believe we are going to become friends, for I felt a great sympathy towards you from the very first.... It is just like in the trenches, before Sebastopol.... See, my dear Moscowitch, I who usually am good for nothing, who am endowed with only a modest activity, I wish, in the name of this common friend, who will be more than a friend for you, to help your noble ambitions, like a brother. You must attain everything: love and glory must crown your genius."

Moscowitch breathed deeply.

"Ah! how happy I am to have met you!"

"Why," Entragues modestly returned, "I think you will not have to repent it. There are so few people capable of understanding; one usually finds only envy, jealousy, stupidity, conceit, and indifference when one is born under a very favorable star. Come, where shall we begin? You know that I can in no way directly intervene to further your marriage. Just acquaint me with what takes place and I will give you advice on the conduct to be followed. You will come to see me; we shall deliberate like a counsel of war; we shall examine the condition of the place; we shall make plans; we shall leave nothing to chance, and we will be victors. Have no doubts upon this. Do you know her long?"

"Since last winter. Some Russian friends gave me a letter of introduction to Madame la comtesse d'Aubry, who introduced me one evening to Madame Magne. I suddenly felt that my life had found its goal."

"It was a sort of thunderbolt?"

"I know that word, thunderbolt," Moscowitch complacently remarked. "No, a sudden attraction, rather. I saw her and loved her—that is all."

"And you did not confess your love till long after?"

"Later, two or three months afterwards. But I believe she had already perceived my sentiments, for she was not surprised to hear me express them."

"The fact that one loves a woman never astonishes her; it is the contrary that surprises her."

"Yes, she had divined my state of mind."

"Oh! they always divine, and that is why confessions always find them so calm. So she allowed you to come to see her?"

"Yes, and I did; but one finds her so rarely! We met quite often at the home of the countess and I spent a delightful fortnight, oh! very delightful, at the château de Rabodanges, during the month of July. I was to have returned there in September and she, too, was to have returned there, but I had to leave for Russia. I am here only a week. I met her again for the first time this evening. I confess, my dear Monsieur d'Entragues, that your entrance in the room was very disagreeable to me. I repent having had this wicked sentiment, but I could not guess that I had before me a friend so ... so...."

"So useful," Entragues finished. "Friends should be useful. That is their purpose. Then, at Rabodanges?"

"It was delightful. I cannot find another word. It was there she did my portrait. It is quite good, only there is no resemblance. I think she was making sport of me that day, for why should she give me a pointed beard instead of this national cut of which I am proud, and which I shall certainly never change. Besides, thanks to retouchings, the very features do not belong to me. She began by copying my figure and ended by designing a dream."

"Was it a sketch?" Entragues asked, amused at this cruel feminine irony.

"Yes, but she etched it the following day, for you know she has a real talent in that direction. She made two copies in my presence, gave me out and then used the same copper plate to elaborate a fantastic landscape where my head became a tree, cloud, grass, I know not what. This figure, which at least I had inspired, I have lost, and despite everything, I deplore its loss because of the inscription."

"That is regrettable," Entragues coldly said, "for without speaking of the sentiment which doubles the price of things, this almost unique sketch had a value because of its rarity and curiosity. If it ever fell into my hands—for things go astray and are found again—I do not truly know if I would surrender it to you. I have a collector's taste."

"It is with this portrait as with its author," replied Moscowitch, with a sudden menacing violence. "I believe it was in the works of a Spanish poet that I once read: 'I love your love more than your life.'"

Entragues was tempted to say: "I possess this sketch, and I have no intention of returning it to you, my friend." What would the consequences be? A duel. But this manner of treating life roughly and questioning the fates was truly quite naive. Sixtine would probably belong to the victor; at least, it would have happened thus in barbarous times. These days, the vanquished have attractions. They inspire pity and the gods are often wrong. "Would I not love her enough to risk my life? Life means nothing to me: if I had any doubts on the matter, I would prove the contrary by quitting it. Moscowitch would willingly fight; but he is a simple soul, while I am very complicated."

Aloud, he continued:

"A woman who inspires such a passion is vanquished in advance. But you must master yourself, so as not to be compromised. Do not see her too often, nor too long at one time. Let her understand that you suffer and that the more cruel she is, the more you suffer. Keep enough presence of mind to remain an exact observer, and then, some fine day, thrust the knife into her neck, crying: 'I suffer too much, be merciful.' She yields and you are happy, unless your imagination has exceeded reality. This happens; then one misses *il tempo de' dolci sospiri*. Oh! you need not fear this weakness; you are robust and she is beautiful. There are other ways of reaching the same end; what I give you is the surest. It is the procedure of physical love, I confess, but no other mimicry affects a woman to a greater degree. Before all, they wish to be desired; the rest comes or does not come, it is an addition. It is the cement which joins the stones, but the Cyclopean constructions dispensed with it quite easily and were not the less solid. Like the block of granite, the strength of the body is the base of all: one must promise marvels of solidity and the idea of duration, of eternal duration, will soon rise. He who gives this impression does not find women inhuman, and he who transforms it into fine and good sensations, during the hours of maturity, has nothing to fear from infidelity. Ah! you are fortunate, Moscowitch; you are a Hercules!"

"You speak," said the Russian, "as if I should dissemble. But this passion, at once ideal and physical, I truly feel and if I say that I suffer I shall not be lying."

"All the better, for sincerity is a mighty wonder-worker, but you would be able to say nothing and, through modesty, you would conceal your sufferings. I merely offer you the means of not suffering, of not loving in vain. Ah! the futile loves, the deceitful tortures of vain desire: tears—good grain sown on the sands!"

"Yes," Moscowitch answered, "all who weep are not consoled. I thank you and understand you. You, too, have the religion of human suffering."

"I!" Hubert wanted to cry, jestingly. But why wound this humanitarian mystic? He simply answered:

"Grief is inevitable, but far from being evil, it is the very honor of humanity and the supreme reason of existence. We suffer in order to be less ugly, and that, in the vulgarity of our animal flesh, there may be an esthetic illusion. Joys are unacceptable and repulsive which have in them no promise of suffering: two lovers, in their sports, make a charming spectacle because they tread on the fragile trap-door of an oubliette, full of stakes and hooks. Intellectual desires, in the same way, are interesting in that they surely lead to the horrors of deception or doubt. Try, then, you who are a poet and a creator of souls, to induce the esthetic thrill in your audience with the picture of a perfect happiness: joy is illogical, and, since the illogical is the essential cause of laughter, joy causes laughter. This might, nevertheless, serve in the fifth act as an unexpected punishment. Could you not show a happy knave just by inflicting upon him the most degrading punishment possible to a man? Happy, while he dreams infinitely of the contempt residing in the word, 'happy'!"

"Yet," Moscowitch answered, "we do nothing else but pursue happiness."

"Oh!" Entragues rejoined, "that is a pastime. We know quite well that we shall never reach it.

"I believe," the Russian said, "that you judge humanity by your own sentiments."

"I think so too," Entragues answered, "but the contrary would be the more surprising. With whose brain would you have me think, if not with my own?"

They separated, after having arranged a rendezvous. Moscowitch, on the day after the morrow or the following day, would call for Entragues at his home, and together they would go to *la Revue spéculative*.

CHAPTER XIX

NEW SUGGESTIONS

"Le fol n'a Dieu."
Epilogue des Contes d'Eutrappei.

"What a painful evening!" thought Hubert, after returning to his home. "What nonsense I have had to think, what platitudes to hear, what stupid remarks to bray? And in what a language! Just so the practical part of my talk be not useless! I count on brutality blended with much weeping: Sixtine will be irritated or bored, and the Russian will disappear from our life. Yes, our life, I have rights upon this woman, those rights of mutual intelligence. We understand each other; with a little attention and verbal caresses, I can acquire a pleasant antenuptial position near her. She is not one of those who are dominated by a perpetual appetite of the flesh and I believe that her delicacy would regard as shameful the very idea of yielding to force. Ah! in short, I do not know her: the plan I have given Moscowitch is perhaps good. Yes, one can never know, but if he adopts it he will have an air of insincerity and she will perceive it."

He was less philosophical on the morrow, and, in a moment of ill-humor, gave himself this alternative which had for an instant occupied him the evening before: Either he would be completely disinterested in Sixtine, or he would become her lover within twenty-four hours. "I cannot play the rôle of a companion to Moscowitch, I cannot admit such a possibility in my life—he or I. What! will those dear arms I have clasped around my neck in dreams caress the Austrian beard of this dramatist? I do not even wish to give expression to my jealousy: in himself, Moscowitch is only another person. Thus, shall another person have those lips and eyes and hair? Vulgar plaints of a vulgar jealous person: to what details do I apply my imagination? How the obscene image possesses me! So one must come to this point, and that is why I love her—for that alone! Bravo! words are useful: with words one analyzes everything, one destroys and sullies everything. Since it is this, I no longer wish it. Valentine plays the beast prettily, and what more do I want! She is sly as a succuba and charming in her ways, and what more do I want! Her caresses have a profuse generosity: her heart is on her hand and on her lips, and what more do I want!"

He took a walk, despite the cold, through the bare and muddy alleys of the Luxembourg, among the shivering statues and silent trees.

"If desire," he thought once more, "permits me—even in thought—the freedom of choice, what is the good of loving, or do I really and truly love? I would perhaps need, like a woman, possession to free me of my doubts. I am afraid lest, after its first blossoming, my temperament grow effeminate and give way, corroded by the rust of a devouring indecision. After my ideas, I analyze my sentiments: the air is becoming unbreathable. I thought that a passion would have refashioned the synthesis of my will; it is too late—the elements, dispersed, have become irreconcilable; here I am, approaching the state of a fakir who, with arms uplifted to an empty sky, immobile and with feet firmly pressed against the ground, dreams of the life he will no longer live. Thinking is not living; living is feeling. Where am I? I wished to penetrate the essence of each thing; I saw that there was nothing but movement, and the world, reduced to an indivisible force, vanished: I expected to double my sensations by dividing them, and I have seen them annihilated. There is nothing worth the lifting of a finger tip: one's reason reduces everything to a vague stirring of cerebral atoms, to a little inward bluster."

As he whispered in the gloomy silence of the vast garden, the words took flight, leaving only a murmuring trace of their passage. It required an effort for him to reseize the logic of his complaints:

"Yes, I was in doubt. Well! I believe that I have cast it beyond the previous limits." This satisfaction of the author cheered him: "So, I shall write about it, I shall show how this little inward bluster, which is nothing, contains everything, how, with the support of a single sensation always the same and distorted from its very inception, a brain isolated from the world can create a world for itself. My Adorer will show whether it is necessary, for the purpose of living, to mingle with surrounding complications. But it is only an experiment and my real work will be this: a being born with the complete paralysis of all his senses, nothing functioning but the brain and the digestive apparatus. This being has no knowledge of external things since, even the sensitiveness of the skin is absent. A miracle, electric or otherwise, partially cures him; he learns to talk and relates his cerebral life: it is just like other lives. It is necessary to find the point of departure, to find, at least, a medical example."

While reflecting, he recognized that his scorn of materialism was leading him a little far: it was hurling him into absurdity. Yet, such an imagination seemed less stupid than the psychical negation of the one group and the dualism of the other. The spiritualists, in fact, did not inspire him with less wrath: these bastards of Theology and Common Sense really formed the most obnoxious hybrid of all the human flora. Of all the outrages which the ignorant pour like a shower of mud on all who think, this class especially offended him and nothing irritated him so much as to hear grouped as idealists, without distinction, all those who do not admit the theories of Büchner, in science, or those of Zola, in literature.

"Ah! I grow angry against ignorance; that is worse than warring with stupidity. And then, among those who do not know are some who would like to know: it is not their fault. A few suffice, besides: only the summits count. It is on the mountains that formerly the annunciatory beacons blazed."

This last reflection was sufficiently disinterested: he willingly thought of himself as a summit, but he also knew that no beacon would ever burn there. The world was not ready to hear any great tidings he cared to announce. Without doubt, like others, he had come too late or too early. The ears would be stopped up if he opened his mouth, for he could only repeat the vain speech of the prophets: Nisi *Dominus aedificaverit domun, in vanum laboraverunt qui aedificant earn*....

"Hello! what are you doing alone, walking like an inspired person?"

"Ah! my dear Calixte, I am bored to death."

"What about spending the evening together?" asked Heliot. "You know, I am hardly entertaining, but we will talk."

"Agreed," said Entragues, taking his friend's arm, "I cling to you, as a castaway to a spar."

"But," returned Calixte laughing, "I am in no wise the partial result of a shipwreck. I ride the sea quite well, the mast is firmly planted, the hull is sound ... come, embark and don't treat me like a wreck. Now, listen, I am going to return and get rid of this cumbersome portfolio; I will get some verses I want to show you, then we will go to your home and you will also read me some slightly symbolic pages, eh?"

They discussed the value of the words with which the modern schools of writers distinguish themselves. The symbolists, according to Entragues, usurped their name; one never makes a symbol purposely, unless one is dedicated to this career as the fabulists to the fable. For him the symbol was the summit of art, conquered only by those who had placed upon it a statue which was superhuman and which yet had a human appearance, containing an idea in its form.

"Now," he continued, "in Milton's Satan you have a symbol, in de Vigny's *Moïse* you have a symbol, in Villiers' *Hadaly* you have a symbol. The symbol is a soul made visible: the type is only the resume or the epitome of a character."

"Your definition is not clear. It seems to me that what you take for the symbol is rather to be called synthesis."

"No, synthesis is found, indeed, in the symbol—it is the final process; if synthesis has not been preceded by an analysis—it matters not whether it be brief or long provided it be exact—there is no symbol, because there is no life."

"Say rather that every psychological masterpiece contains a symbol."

"Perhaps," conceded Entragues. "Would a symbolist then signify a fabricator of masterpieces?"

"At least that is quite an interesting ideal and I believe you will not disclaim it. You don't worry about the public any more than I do; you would rather please ten select persons than please everybody, to the exclusion of the ten."

"Evidently. We are not actors and the applause do not make us beam with joy. But if we write neither to win universal approbation nor to earn money, we become truly incomprehensible."

"Write for your mistress," said Calixte.

"I have none," said Entragues.

"Write for the Madonna of Botticelli," said Calixte.

"That is what I am doing," said Entragues.

"A lovely and noble confident. Do you remember what the page says in the *Gitana*? I know it by heart. It is the portrait of our mistress, since it is that of poetry, Listen to it in the stately language of Cervantes: '*La poesia es una bellissima doncella, casta, honesta, discreta, aguda, retirada, y que se contien en las limites de la discrecion mas alta: es amiga de la soledad, las fuentes la entretien, los prados la consuelan, los arboles la desenojan, los flores le alegran; y finalmente deleyta y ensena a quantos con ella communican.*'"

Their talk often ended thus, by the recollection of an old impression, in mystic and shy plaints. Calixte was gentle towards life, which had not shown him the same clemency. No one knew what he sought, excepting the fine editions of old poets and the mysterious modern prints: his disdain of all vainglory was more sincere than that of Entragues, in whom heredity determined a dim need of social domination. Entragues strove to scorn life. During the long and painful reckonings of his tutelage, he had undergone, without external revolt, the humiliation of a lowly situation, a horror of the forced fabrication of worthless copy for miserly publishers. The verdict of several lawsuits had despoiled him of the relics of his patrimony; but he would have consented to a Castilian wretchedness rather than abandon his dream. He wished to regild his name, and, encircled by glory, he hated the present, as an obstacle, but he would have liked to assume the existence that was due him, to put it on like a ducal cloak, without astonishment, with the satisfaction of a lord returning to his domains. He was waiting; nothing would have surprised him, but neither did the nothing surprise him: hence, the infinite contradictions of his character and conduct. He knew his nature and had applied to himself, with a joy which revealed the triplicity of his soul, this line of Dante:

Che sensa speme vivemo in disio.

"And without hope live in desire." His triplicity, a quite elementary scholastic division, he thus explained: a soul that wills, a soul that knows the uselessness of willing, a soul that watches the struggle of the other two and writes the Iliad of it.

He had no naïveté, save perhaps in his rare unfortunate crises, for in his normal state his proud indifference of principle saved him from anger and its consequences. Thus, his indignation against Moscowitch had become deadened after the first thought of vengeance, and he was the man, on matters that did not touch the essentials, to give up a thing in despair, send the handle after the ax. But he was also the man to lift and unite the fallen instrument. He was the man to do the contrary of what he pretended to do, but as his acts were a spectacle to himself, and the most amusing of all spectacles, he never let it sadden him beyond measure. He knew himself full of the unexpected and liked it: ah! without this he surely would have been wearied, for the rest of the world unrolled itself to his wearied eyes but as a circus performance, truly too monotonous; the world was peopled by vague and distant phantoms thrown on the eternally trod course.

Calixte was much more simple: all dream, all faith, all spontaneity. No one could guess at the aim of his movements, and, in short, he had no other aim than movement itself. Older than Entragues by five or six years, and having attained a certain renown as a stylist and delicate thinker, he was unconcerned with it; he always kept the tone and the manners of a beginner, carried his manuscripts here and there, preferably to the little new reviews, not, like others, with the purpose of lording it there, but rather from a need of silence, not to have to discuss, to demonstrate, by a necessary charlatanry, the merit of a work.

He earned little, because of his indifference, for he could easily have won a lucrative position in journalism. But he loved, above all things, to work freely and with dignity.

His disdain of life was naive: he did not know life, just as one is ignorant of analytical chemistry, and he no more felt the inclination to live in the modern fashion than to shut himself up in a cellar with retorts; either of these careers seemed equally absurd in his estimation. Some dream figures—creatures encountered in the pages of Shakespeare or Calderon, personal creations—sufficed to people his days. He considered his illusions the only beings not endowed with the melancholy spirit of contradiction; he loved them, and he loved Entragues and all the intelligent persons who discussed things politely and without prolixity.

He was said to be as chaste as a Franciscan monk: he disclaimed such an eccentricity. A pretty and short love affair did not displease him: he enjoyed a woman's grace more than her beauty, her childishness more than her sex. He considered nervous disorders, so aggravated by the complacency of deteriorated writers, as repugnant maladies that were anti-harmonious, and he shunned dark and thin women, who smell fresh flesh, like the ogre.

They entered, as had been agreed, the home of Entragues, who read the following tale to his friend.

CHAPTER XX

THE TWENTY-EIGHTH OF DECEMBER

"... L'une meurt, l'autre vit, mais la
morte parfois se venge d'être morte."
Anonymous.

At the corner of the fire-place, in the cool chamber, they were talking affectingly, for it was the hour when their closed lips, with a tacit agreement, were opening the door to their imprisoned souls. Sidoine had courted Coquerette for two months. He did not speak to her of earth and sky, nor of the charming destiny of lovers who fly away on wings, in the estival purple of evenings, towards the luminous heights; he spoke to her of new dresses and the Auteuil races, of the Opera, of the Salon, of the street, of the Boulogne wood, and of the *Revue des Deux-Mondes*: she understood him and found him witty.

Sidoine amused himself in loving listlessly. Having greatly suffered during a whole year, he felt the need of diversion, of playing light-heartedly and of kissing, with a smile, a blond head and two blue eyes.

Coquerette also amused herself. She had a husband, amiable but *bourgeois*, a member of a club of the second order and of several councils. He often played baccarat: cards were lenient with his purse and the Bourse with his pocketbook. She did not understand him, but she respected him greatly and in the matrimonial hour did not pout at him more than two out of three times.

A husband is a father, a brother; he kisses your lips instead of kissing your brow; he sleeps with you, because it is customary, or because the apartments are too small; and he pays you an intimate visit because you are within easy reach, and you must have a child, or two, when business is good.

A lover is a child, something you have yourself created, he belongs to you, you can play with him, fondle him, rock him, kiss him, beat him, console him, caress him, punish him, scold him, deprive him of dessert, make him hold pins when you dress, send him to bed at eight o'clock.

You become a little girl again, you have a doll: ah! it is altogether different.

Coquerette did not have a child, she wished to play, and Sidoine asked for nothing better.

The moment, however, was grave: they were going to pass to the other side of the river, and it was necessary to jump into the water and swim to the other bank, shoulder against shoulder. Afterwards they bask in the sun on the green lawn and, recovered from emotions, they enjoy fine moments, gathering pleasing flowers; and with what delight they return to bathe in the river so terrible not long ago, now so gentle, so mild, so tenderly murmuring.

He took Coquerette's hands and began to kiss her fingers one after the other with a gracefulness which charmed her; she grew tender at such delicacy of sentiment, the poor darling! It did not take a much stronger wind to disperse the last birds still chattering among the branches; she suddenly felt her heart grow light, for never had her spouse had the idea of such an exquisite caress, "and since he never thought of it, I really must love another. Can one reasonably demand that a woman deprive herself of such delights? If my husband is incapable, that is not my fault!"

Sidoine continued, having found this means of dispensing with speech and counting equally on finding, thanks to a few minutes of this practice, the means of dispensing with thought.

He recommenced with the little finger and Coquerette had the enraptured eyes of Psyche under the first kiss of love.

Sidoine kissed the little finger on the second phalanx, for he had distributed the round of his kisses on the nails, at first, then on the first joint.

He kissed the little finger and at the same instant there returned to his lips, and this time almost terrifying, these syllables that had already been inwardly pronounced:

"The magnificence!"

Coquerette thought he said: "I love you, little finger of Coquerette," and she was content.

Sidoine kissed the second joint of the ring-finger of Coquerette, and this other word issued from his lips:

"Funereal!"

Coquerette thought he said: "I love you, annular finger of Coquerette," and she was content.

Sidoine kissed the joint of the middle finger of Coquerette, and he said nothing.

Coquerette thought the gentle familiar lizard was climbing along her hand, along her wrist, along her bare arm: "Gracious! how far will he go? I am going to keep my eyes closed, I will see very well."

But the caress stopped, startled; Sidoine stood up, pale; he gazed at the bed as one gazes at an unexpected and melancholy spectacle.

"The magnificence is funereal, and my heart is terrified."

The words had joined and from the magic union was born the real unity contained in their elements.

It really was a funereal magnificence:

Three wax-tapers were lighted at the heads of the bed and in their gleam the white figure seemed to be smiling at angels, like little children in their cradles. A great black crucifix appeared under her crossed hands; flowers were scattered, roses on her breast, lilies on her body and violets at her feet.

"No, she is not dead!" cried Sidoine, kneeling near his mistress. "Speak, you are not dead? Open your eyes, if you recognize me? What have you done? Why these lights, why all these flowers, you are going to give her a headache."

It was just a year, the twenty-eighth of December last, since he had come to her home: it was the same funereal magnificence and he had uttered the same words, shed the same tears.

He took the hand of the dead woman and raised it to his lips, but the affright of a sudden shock threw him to the ground: she was cold.

Coquerette, her large blue eyes wide opened, had followed with amazement the phases of the terrifying vision. She knew Sidoine's history and understood that a stroke of love madness had touched her friend at the-very hour of the poignant anniversary.

The little frivolous and laughing woman felt a strange thrill. She rose palpitating, threw herself upon Sidoine, as a lioness on her prey, and bit him on the cheek.

Sidoine opened his eyes:

"Ah! you are mine, mine only, mine," cried Coquerette kissing, bewildered, the impression of her teeth, "I have marked you with my sign, you belong to me. I love you, Sidoine, I love you even to death. Ah! I have never felt anything like it!"

She lifted him up, made him sit down, placed herself at his feet.

"She is dead," said Sidoine, still giddy, but recovered, "she is dead, but I will love her eternally."

"And me? And me?"

Sidoine did not reply.

"And me? And me?"

Sidoine gently kissed her brow.

"And me? And me?"

"She is dead!" said Sidoine.

"I will die," said Coquerette.

"For what reason?" asked Sidoine.

"So as to be loved," said Coquerette.

CHAPTER XXI

THE MYSTIC BARK

"L'épouvantable misère de ceux qui vivent
sans amour."
Rusbrock l'Admirable,
De la Jouissance chaste.

"Do you know, Madame, that Monsieur Moscowitch has the firm intention of marrying you?"

"That is quite natural."

"Yes, but what do you say to it?"

"It is agreeable to me."

"Then," asked Entragues, "why did you not let me know?"

"Ah! you would like to have the cards stacked. You do not wish to waste your time? At first, not any more than yourself, Monsieur Moscowitch never asked more than the pleasure of seeing me."

"He is fascinating."

"Isn't he?" returned Sixtine. "He pleases me very much and I believe that with him I shall never be bored."

"Ah! you are quite perverse, but perhaps that is why I love you."

"Perverse, because I do not wish to be bored!"

"No, boredom is the terror of every woman, and they commit half of their crimes to escape its claws. But it is useless. Boredom, impassive, smokes his houka and maintains his slaves. I well know that passion is stronger than he is, but you are incapable of loving."

"No more than another," Sixtine nonchalantly said, "and, besides all I ask is to be given the chance. I have already told you I was dough waiting for the hands of the kneader; and, after all I can not fashion myself alone. But are you coming to warble such poor ditties of jealousy, and in such a vulgar style. I believed you had more disdain and a richer vocabulary. Ah, fie! to sing such a romanza to me: 'You are incapable of loving.' Well, Monsieur, to use your language, I am at least capable of being loved. You seem to think that in love there is a category of capacities as in the time of Louis-Philippe? Would it be a special string that the cithara lacks? All the human instruments are complete and even women have spare strings, if you care to know. But skillful citharists are rare and most men only know how to direct the preliminary chord of the instrument from which they pretend to draw music. Please speak to me in the language of a logician, since that is your intellectual profession, and do not imagine that I am a boarding-school girl who will feel herself burning with love, through a very noble spirit of contradiction, at the very moment when a man presents her adroit inaninity: 'You are incapable of loving.' For you are perhaps very skillful and capable, oh! very capable of demonstrating the patent lack of logic in my feminine deductions. But, question me!"

"I get," said Entragues, "much pleasure in listening to you. Your voice is sweet."

"This time," he thought, "thanks to the mutual impertinences with which we are offending each other, things will end very well or very badly. She is very much unnerved and my own mental state lacks poise. We are going to reach, it is to be hoped, a surprising result."

As she was silent, he resumed:

"There are instruments irremediably out of tune, like those which undergo the humidity of solitude; but it is not such a great disaster—you have but to change the strings."

"A turn of the peg perhaps might suffice," said Sixtine, "and first of all, a ray of sunshine."

That word went straight to his heart. Yet the voice which had pronounced it was cold and brittle with irony, but he only kept its sense and saw rising before him, under the form of a sorrowful woman with imploring gestures, the very figure of Abandonment. Her fingers dropped arrows at his feet, he was naively touched:

"I have offended you, forgive me."

"Yes," Sixtine said, "you have been spiteful and it has hurt me. Let us become good friends, while awaiting something better, if it is to be our destiny that I put my hand in your hand forever. But do rot vent your anger against a weak woman, unfortunate enough already in not knowing what she wants. You have no cause to be jealous, and besides," she smiled, but not mischievously, "you have not the right, my friend."

He had placed a knee on the ground before her and held her hand in his hands, without pressing it, with precaution, like a fragile and precious porcelain.

"Here I am," he thought, "in the attitude of Sidoine before Coquerette, I have but to bring these fingers and nails to my lips to complete the resemblance, making allowances for the different natures of the two women. Coquerette, that capricious and laughing child, might experience a sudden but momentary change of nature. Her very sincere passion for Sidoine will last as long as Sidoine does not respond —perhaps a few days. As Sidoine seeks no more in this pretty little woman than a diverting intrigue, he is quite capable of yielding on the very evening, despite the shocked nerves, when this would be but out of human respect. In that case, Coquerette's passion would not be protracted: the wood would blaze and quickly become a little heap of ashes. But how singular! at the very moment of the thunderbolt, and during all those surprising electric effects, Coquerette is the woman to give Sidoine, if he quite openly scorned her, a truly great and real proof of love: she would throw herself through the window, if no revolver came to her hand. I could write this sequel, or some other, for there are two or three equally logical denouements in every love story.... Where was I? Sixtine is quite different from Coquerette...."

A long silence had followed the last words of Sixtine, during which Entragues, without ceasing to be absorbedly interested in the present, could nevertheless not curb his analytical imagination.

"I know it, I know it too well," answered Hubert between two attitudes, "but you say bitter things with such sweetness and charm that they delight me like tender caresses. The future, where you let me glimpse the possibility of joy, appears to me like the thought and imagination of dawn to a poor pilgrim who has stayed too long in the horrors of a black forest...."

"Imagination, if such is your pleasure, my friend; but strike and the spring will gush. Strike boldly, make way to my heart, make my blood flow like a stream, and let me fall into the murderer's arms, dying of joy and dying of love. I would like, I would like...."

"Ah! tell me just what I would like," Sixtine continued inwardly, "evoke my will before me, let me see it with my eyes, let me touch it with my hands. You can do it, you should be able, since you are a man!..."

She waited a second: the aura of a nervous stroke hovered nearby and played along her spine, the swelling ball traveled along her neck; her fingers thrilled in the hand of Entragues, she felt the imperious necessity of shunning all contact and, suddenly rising, she went to her piano and feverishly played an incoherent piece of music which saved her.

"She is strange," thought Entragues. "One might say that she was going to let herself go and suddenly she flies away from peril. She never loses her head and I should truly applaud the advice which a diabolic inspiration made me give this poor Moscowitch. She is not a Coquerette, she can master herself, but on the day when the river shall have been crossed, shoulder against shoulder, she will be united to her lover as iron to iron under the hammer of the good smith:

"Love, good smith of hearts,
Hammer, hammer,
Hammer two by two the hearts,
Hammer, hammer,
Love, good smith of hearts!"

He hummed this verse, improvised at the end of a rhythm that sang under Sixtine's fingers. Verses, welcome phrases, fine periods rose to his lips according to the cadence of the music and with the words came ideas, curious ideas with which he had no acquaintance, plans of romances, metaphysical romances, interesting views on himself, on his friends, on love, on politics. During the hour that Sixtine was at the piano, he lived through several days of a full deep life, and when the music paused, Hubert felt a violent arrest of thought which seized his heart and brain, just as an extreme and sudden transition from warm to cold seizes the flesh and marrow.

"Now," said Sixtine, half turning on her stool, "to prove to you that you are still a person I trust, despite your blunder, I will tell you some fragments of my life. Do not take it for a confession, nor for a secret, nor for an avowal; it is nothing else than goodness of heart on my part, and the desire to satisfy your curiosity. I hardly like to explain my past miseries, and I really believe, besides, that no one has ever seen the spectacle, unless it be the countess and a dead friend, dear and always dear in memory, of Sixtine tearing aside the veil of Isis."

"Your past," said Entragues, "is as sacred to me as a religious mystery. I do not question that you have always behaved like a woman endowed with natural dignity...."

"Precisely," interrupted Sixtine, "I am and was a woman, and I committed the crimes of a woman who does not know the meaning of the word 'duty.' I was taught it, I forgot it, never having understood it."

"If you have forgotten it," said Entragues, "I will not try to have you learn it anew, before knowing you better. Duty for me consists in doing my work and cutting down all the obstacles of life; I do not know what duty is to another."

"Yes, you are an intellectual. Some men are and many might become intellectuals, but it is not possible for a woman. Those women who have the air of interesting themselves in things of the mind do so only through pretense of imitation. The silver circle of sensation clasps them and sentiment remains sentiment to them. I have been told this and you are right in thinking that I could not have found it out myself; besides, it is a matter of indifference to me, since, like other women, I seek only happiness."

"And you are not happy."

"No, but I can be. I live for that: it is my work, I shall pursue it to my last hour and I am quite tranquil."

"You will give me your secret," said Entragues.

"In a moment," said Sixtine. "If an adventure like the first came to me, it would be myself, not the other, who would die. You have perhaps learned that when any one speaks to me of love, it is not only the peace of my heart which is at stake, but the light of my eyes. This should give me, I believe, the right of choosing: well, I will not choose. Thus, I shall have nothing with which to reproach myself, if I am shipwrecked. I shall have usurped neither the speaking-trumpet nor the helm, I will be the passenger who sleeps in the ship and sails with closed eyes. And to think," she added, as if speaking to herself, "that it needs but eight days for me to be at sea, embarked towards reefs, in a capsizing ship and under an inexperienced command! Isn't that what awaits me? I prefer therefore not to set sail, life is not painful to me; but I shall depart, for some one will lift me from the ground and some one's arms ... whose?... will place me on the cushions amid the rolling waves.... Ah! I am capable of having a very happy voyage, a voyage of real pleasure through oceans full of sunshine with a calm and cool port, and smiles of good souls, for my destination, to the very end...."

"It shall be so," said Entragues.

The tragic simplicity of this woman who vouch-safed to confess herself, affected him as much as a beautiful sunrise or as perfect prose in splendid print. At this moment, he no longer felt any love for her; the impression was wholly literary, and with a remnant of conscience, he cursed himself for this blasphemy. Yet he noticed this: the metaphorical developments with which Sixtine had indicated her conception of the future were analogous to the images which had haunted him one day in a similar state of-mind. A fugitive state, doubtless, but one whose birth, though occasional, revealed secret agreements between their souls. If not the joys of union a great devotion was at least possible, and it is much that two beings be qualified for the same sufferings, and that if life strike one heart the other be wounded. This transitory thought led him back to love: his arms, by a sudden loosened spring, opened and, if she had fallen into them, they would have closed again on the infinite. But he was too late by several minutes: there is a very tiny space between perceived sensation and analyzed sensation: it is there that the ironic "Too Late" dwells.

Sixtine answered:

"What do you know? Could you, yourself, promise me, on your life, that the morrows will not bring me the disillusion of your past days? Will you make such a promise?"

The sun had had its day, and the sky, by slow diminutions, darkened. Red, green and yellow fires blazed on the stream.

Languid under its trappings, lightly rocked by the eddy, a slow bark drew near and anchored at the quay. The stones were all covered with heavy rugs, as were the granite steps and the pavement to the foot-path where the carriage stopped. Torch carriers lined the road to the bark: by their flickering flames, the golds and purples of the draperies brightened and the water of the river assumed the color of garnets and topazes.

They were alone. Holding each other's hand, they walked in silence, both garbed in black and resembling shadows.

When they stepped on the plank, they looked and smiled at each other. They departed alone, they departed together, and yet each saw in the other's eye the melancholy of voyagers.

The bark put to sea, the torches were extinguished: in the night there was again but one lantern on the water of the stream.

"Yes," said Entragues.

Sixtine shuddered.

"Yes," repeated Entragues, "if you love me!"

Sixtine continued:

"There's a story intermingled with much prattling.... I am speaking for myself."

"I deserve my part of the blame," returned Entragues.

And to himself he added:

"If you love me! I have the air of laying down my conditions. What cowardice made me pronounce these humiliating syllables! I, too, have spoiled everything. I had only to say 'yes'! And that was my whole thought, it was my true thought. Yet I love you, Sixtine, I really love you without conditions, you see! Ah! you will end by understanding it."

Sixtine observed him:

"Ah! my poor friend, will you never understand me, then?"

She said loud:

"But we must end.... It is because I have some modesty in baring myself in this way.... After all.... No, enough for to-day ... another time .... Please leave me, now, if you wish to please me ... without questions ... and without fear ... you will come to-morrow. Good-by, my friend."

CHAPTER XXII

THE SIMONIAC

"La malle bouche, elle a raté si traistre
Qu'elle a baisé et vendu nostre maistre."
Charles de la Huetrie,
Contreblason de la Bouche.

Hubert had no desire whatever to think, but it is not given to all persons to be able to regulate cerebral activity and to dismiss the serious affairs until the morrow. Neither the reading of a naturalistic novel, nor meditation upon the most abtruse propositions and scholia of the contemporary thinkers, nor the contemplation of the eternal verities, prevented him from bewailing his recent foolish behavior.

Ah! how well he judged things from a distance, how well he saw *what he should have done.* No one had to a higher degree his presence of mind at the foot of the staircase.

Immediate analysis was always slightly confused and did not force any precise conclusions. Without doubt, it was always three or four minutes after the occasion had passed that he was able to unravel the thoughts and the mental reservations of his partner, and by the forth minute he already knew *what he should have done* at the first second, but he never knew it so pertinently as after a night's sleep.

No disturbance of his heart had ever prevented him from sleeping; he thanked heaven for having granted him lucid mornings.

The more he thought, this morning, the more the moving sands of indecision shifted.

Having taken an awkward step, he had seen how pernicious action had proved to him; to wait was sterile: it is like the sower of pebbles who, pausing along the fields in spring, is astonished not to see any germination.

"Well," thought Hubert, "one cannot know, everything happens and the absurd especially. I should be pleased if some miracle would occur in my favor. We shall see this evening, and," he added, smiling at himself, "the following days."

Impatient for the night, and fearing the surliness of the hours, he went out in search of casual diversion.

The street was inclement. The quays, swept by a sharp and humid wind, stood out gloomily under their closed boxes, truly an unfavorable sight to those restless plunderers of knowledge. What becomes of the disconsolate vagabonds, amateurs of printed foolishness, in those days of enforced idleness? He perceived one, with sad eyes and weary movements, who was examining the sky, holding out against the storm and waiting for a lull. Entragues knew him: he was an old man of letters who spent his days here. No book was unknown to him, he dipped into all of them, saluted them with a smile, but purchased only those which concerned the Auvergne, his native country. In a vast garret he had fifteen thousand books of this kind and did not despair of doubling the number.

Entragues wished to lead him away from these desolate banks; he resisted, like a lover who has decided to sleep across the bolted door of his mistress.

This constancy pleased Entragues.

"Just come as far as the rue de Richelieu. There is a big Moorish room where you can also find some books, and you are in shelter."

"Yes, it is all right, but you can't take them with you."

Entragues left him at this word whose bitterness he understood, for he too belonged to those who can only read with pleasure the books that one owns. Books, women, pictures, horses, statues and the rest, the very grass and trees and everything one enjoys can only be half-enjoyed if it is not owned. That explains the little success of museums, usually deserted except on rainy Sundays; a great indifference or a great detachment is necessary to bestow enthusiastic feelings on the contemplation of a picture which an imbecile glance will pollute the moment after.

Rue de Richelieu has a special atmosphere which can only be breathed there. As soon as one enters, a little chill strikes the hands and feet, and once installed in the chair and in a numbered place, one feels the cruel feverish embraces of books.

Entragues could not remain seated. He walked along the aisle, examining the heads at his right and the books at his left. Evidently, all those heads believed in knowledge and came here to imbibe books, in which—as one knows—all knowledge is contained. Pliny, too, believed in knowledge, and Paracelsus, and Erasmus, and Salmasius, and where is their knowledge, Villon! It is where your verses shall never go, poor scholar! You knew, and among other things you knew that who-ever dies, "dies in grief." Work, work and some day knowledge, like gall, will rend your heart. Work, if it is necessary to live; that is an excuse, although, according to a certain preface, one must not attach too much value to one's daily bread. But," continued Entragues, "must humanity grow weary intentionally so that there may be amateurs of labor!"

"What, you, Oury? I thought you were in the provinces."

"I made for myself," answered Oury, "a corner of the provinces in Paris, and as you see I am alive, or at least I appear to be so."

"And what are you doing?"

"Nothing."

"What do you mean, nothing? when I find you leaning against the big catalogues!"

"I came here to rest my eyes a little, for I do not work, I watch others work."

"Ah!"

"Yes, I come here each noon and remain till closing time. In summer this takes place at six o'clock, so I do a good day's work. In winter I have hardly time to install myself."

"And you do nothing?"

"No, I wait. I am like the scholar in the legend: I wait until the others leave."

"My dear Oury, your psychology is really interesting. 'I wait until the others leave!' Your device is the very device of humanity. It is admirable, it is the scheme of life. You are a man, Oury, you are the man, you are symbolic."

"Perhaps, but I do not get any vanity from the fact. Yet my existence is singular and I imagine that few creatures will have lived whole days so destitute of incidents. Sit down and we will talk; I really can sacrifice an hour or two to an old friend."

Entragues willingly consented.

"You thought that I was in the provinces?" commenced Oury. "I am a man who has disappeared, but not a provincial. Do you see that gray-haired, very amiable man down there, at the desk. I bow to him, he smiles and offers me a little paper which I take. I also smile, for this paper which is used to ask for a book is useless to me. I do not come here to work, but to watch others work.

"I spend five or six agreeable hours here.

"It is quite different at home in the morning. Time creeps like a serpent, writhes, yawns, bites me, instills me with the cataleptic venom of boredom.

"I sometimes open my window in fine weather and gaze upon the distant trees; other mornings I read Ronsard. Time goes! time goes! No, it lies heavy, useless and tenacious.

"I had two or three months of respite, several years ago.

Paint me, Janet, the beauties of my darling.

"I set out in quest of this visionary portrait. Why had Thomas de Leu not engraved it? He is without an equal in frilling a starched collar, in lengthening ferociously the face of a leaguer, but delicately that of a princess. As this picture does not exist, and I knew it did not exist, I sought it perseveringly, for I was at least sure of never touching the final disillusion with my finger.

"But my weary steed staggered; a whip lashed his croup; I found my princess, painted by Janet, in the Louvre. I recognized her by her long and pale figure, her almond eyes, her large white collar, her slender shape made still more delicate by a pointed bodice, her Mary Stuart chapeau, her gray gloves, her gauntlets, her undeniable Renaissance air. I fell in love with her.

"As I am quite regular in my habits, the princess never failed to appear on the mornings that followed the first vision. She was ever the same, ever the princess. She entered the Louvre, I unfortunately went to the library, for I could neither stop myself nor follow her, so that it was a long time before I knew if it was a hallucination or the tangible reality of a woman endowed with flesh and bones.

"We left each other under the vault where the Egyptian and Assyrian perspectives are situated: she entered by the right and I continued on my way. I might have entered and followed her, doubtless, but the hours spent here are sacred to me: it is true that I do not work, but I might work: I wish, at least, to preserve the possibility of the duty. All that is left of my will has been transmuted into habits: to snap the thread would be to resolve the series of learned movements into an eternal immobility.

"You see that I know myself somewhat. The more I go on, the more I lack initial force. I can continue anything, I can commence nothing. Between the will and the act is a hollow ditch into which I would fall if I attempted to leap it: it is a physical impression.

"One day, finally, my princess appeared in a Van Dyck hat which threw very ugly shadows on her white figure: farewell to my princess painted by Janet! She was a woman like all other women and could not, decidedly, atone for this fault by any other merit.

"That is my adventure.

"I find that life, at bottom, is quite tolerable after the noon hour. I wait for inspiration, I watch others work, and that is an occupation."

"It is an occupation," said Entragues. "Good-by. Are you not coming out with me?"

"Oh, no," Oury replied, "it is impossible. Not before four o'clock."

Entragues left him and continued his walk, seeking some head familiar to his eyes among the bowed skulls. Vain search! Then he withdrew alone, without the companion he would have liked, and strolled up the street as far as the boulevard. Oury had thrown a gloom over him.

Entragues was afraid of growing indifferent because of the confidences of this sad invalid, once an intelligent boy whom his friends had thought destined to write interesting retrospective criticism, a sort of history of the Pleiade, less puerile and braver than that of the doleful Sainte-Beuve. These sicknesses of the will were contagious: he decided to shun this intellectual leper and abolish at once all remembrance of the meeting. A like malady might entrap his nerves and lay low his will in the beaten path of habit; he was not eager for a sojourn, not even for a tourist's excursion, within the borders of madness.

He sauntered along, visited some editorial offices in search of Van Baël, whom he wished to consult on a detail of costume, passed a half hour in an auction room where he bought some ancient silks and a lot of faded church ornaments, ugly, but sacred and smelling of simony.

A simoniac priest had haunted him for years; his was a lean face with malignant eyes, a rigid skeleton-like body, long hands, white hands, supple hands with square nails, hands of a seller of stuffs, hands of one who blesses, hands of a Jew quickly returned into the cloak with the prize of blood. In what century and country lived he?

"To reach some appropriateness of analysis," thought Entragues, while returning to his dwelling, a chasuble on his knees and a great heap of sacerdotal embroideries filling the rest of the carriage, "to instill true life into this simoniac, he should be modern. It would be necessary for me to be able to enter into his church, take a seat some evening and kneel down in his confessional, drinking the wine from his chalice and taking the consecrated wafers from his pyx. Like him I would have to be simoniacal and sacrilegious, Ah! what a test! and like him I would have to feel the irrevocable damnation and daily glorify myself with the opprobrious secret of my lies!"

Sixtine came to his rescue: the red robe rid him of the black robe.

The hour of the meeting, given the evening before, rang.

"Madame has gone out!"

"Ah!"

That was all. Why even open the mouth again?

CHAPTER XXIII

THE ADORER

III. Fumes of Incense

"Il y a un secret, Valérien, que je veux
le dire; j' ai pour amant un ange de Dieu,
qui, avec une extrême jalousie, veille sur
mon corps."
Bréviare romain,
Office de sainte Cécile.

"The incense! The incense!

"What incense there is in the censers!

"What fumes there are in the incense!

"That cloud is pagan, Virgin! Fie! to hide yourself in a cloud in order to love. But why? I see the wings of the angel whose whiteness shines under the fragrant cloud. It is with this, with so little, Virgin I fie! that he has intoxicated you to possess you. And you smile at him, I see your eyes whose splendor shines under the fragrant cloud, in the shadow of the white wings.

"Thou, the immaculate! And for whom is so much purity sullied? For an angel?"

"You fancied it was the Holy Spirit?"—"Yes, the dove pecked my lips and I opened my lips and I gave him the end of my tongue. I speak of the past. It was very pleasant and I have always wanted to begin again."

"Ah! Virgin, fie, you lie like a woman. Doves have no such large wings."—"They are the wings of my mantle."

"Ah? Virgin! Fie! doves have not light feathers."—"But they have, they have! And besides they are not light, *figliuolo*, they are shot-color."

Such aplomb confused Delia Preda. What! a Virgin in whom he had placed his whole confidence, *sub tuum praesidium*!

The colloquy was resumed in this fashion:

"Ah! Virgin! Fie! think of your family, think of your chaste spouse! think of your son! think of God the father! Do you wish to dishonor the creator of heaven and earth? What will become of us, if you awaken his wrath? It is always on us, poor mortals, that his wrath falls, and we will have the plague again."—"*Ecce ancilla Domini!* my friend. I am under the orders of the Most High, and what if it pleases him to send me an angel?"

Della Preda did not know what reply to make, for he was too religious to question the eternal decrees. He contented himself with remarking to the madonna that if the Most High had sent her an angel, it was not apparently to have love with him.

"Ah! Good Lord!" the Novella cried.

"Moreover," continued Delia Preda, "I am at peace, for the angels have no sex. It is merely play. Ah, well! the question is controverted."

"Ah! Good Lord! Ah! Good Lord!" the Novella cried.

"Thus, Saint Ambrose, who has discussed angels at some length, does not pronounce himself in a peremptory way. He notes that some, having transgressed, were thrust 'into the world' and replaced in the celestial concert by the most meritorious virginities. How did they transgress, and must not this expression mean the flesh?..."

"Ah! my angel!" the Novella cried.

"Or perhaps they are epicene, like their name. This opinion was sustained but I believe it heretical, for these vases of purity, finding themselves endowed with two sexes, would have too many temptations. Tertullian, as well as Origen, grants them a body: I know that to be so, and I see what profane use they make of it.

"Ah! I am about to lose all my illusions concerning angels: I must submit the case to the padre who taught me theology....

"If I call to mind my prayer-book, is it not written in the service of Saint-Cecilia: 'Valerian found Cecilia supplicating with an angel in her bed. Cecilia, moreover, had informed him beforehand: 'There is a secret, Valerian, I wish to tell thee: I have an angel of God for a lover; he watches over my body with an extreme jealousy.' Yes, I have read this in my prayer-book, in those holy pages where disrespect should not even appear. I read about holy loves, and of saints also, without a doubt, and these things oppress my heart. Pardon, madonna! Nevertheless you make me suffer and you make me weep; I no longer dare, ashamed of the spectacle which has disturbed my soul, lift my rude eyes towards your beatified eyes. You do what you wish, being a queen, and my only duty is to love, to suffer and to die if you so order it.

"I do not understand at all, but what matter? Do I understand the mystery of the Holy Trinity?

"If you have chosen, like the charming and blest maiden, an angel for lover, it is because it is the function of angels to be the lovers of virgins: it was so ordained by the Lord for all eternity.

"And I, I am unworthy; my body is soiled, twice soiled: since the baptism of your love, madonna, the carnal seductions have prevailed over the grace which your intercession had granted me.

"To a woman, and what a woman! to an infidel, and what an infidel! I have betrayed my body that had been regenerated by the condescension of your gaze, lavished by your tears, purified by your smile, as a scabious rag by the running of the stream and by the rays of sunshine.

"You have punished me, madonna, but should I moan, since I myself have supplicated you to whip my shoulders with the rod. You have punished me well, thanks ... I hate you now, impure and perjured Virgin!

"Dream that I love you for your immaculate candor, and that your virginal skin is spotted with ineffable stains...."

"It can no longer be seen," the Virgin said, "I have a new robe."

"My lord," said Veltro, bowing to the prisoner, "the ceremony is ended and we must return. I have taken it upon myself to prolong the minutes, but orders, my lord, orders ... all the same, the crowning of a madonna is a fine holiday. The Novella is crowned every year at Assumption, and her red robe is changed at the same time; it is the custom. The little poor girls are given the old gown and dresses are made of it. And how proud the little rascals are; after all, it is the custom, you see!"

"Another moment, Veltro, please, my friend?"

After Della Preda had raised his eyes and saw the Novella face to face, radiant in her new purple and without the veil of any cloud, his anguish and bewilderment subsided. All he felt was the agitation that follows an evil dream, like a persistent odor, but suddenly the sensation of blasphemy struck him; it was dim and violent: he swooned and Veltro took him in his arms.

CHAPTER XXIV

THE COLOR OF MARRIAGE

"The dotal husband owes his wife three
nights each month."
Attic Laws.

"Good," Entragues said, as he heard the bell ring. "It is the Russian angel... Ah! I have written a fine blasphemy! '... in his arms.' And to think that for want of understanding, people will tax me with impiety, I who make the Roman breviary my daily reading no less than a clergyman who holds the name of Voltaire as an infamous word."

"My dear Moscowitch, I made you wait. The reason was that I was finishing a phrase and that this phrase ended a chapter."

The Russian angel drank tea while Entragues breakfasted. He spoke little, seeming to hold himself in reserve.

"Have you your manuscripts, your plans, your theories?" asked Entragues.

"My theory," said Moscowitch, "is to make a school of pity out of the theater."

"Orphans, bastards, picked up children, widows, persons condemned to death, serfs of capital, girl mothers, invalids of labor, vagabonds and victims of duty. Well! by dressing them in Russian smocks, by giving the men names ending in itch and the women names ending in ia, with some troikas thrown in, snow, Siberia, a priest or two, policemen in flat caps, some angelic street-walkers, and a studied selection of Darwinian assassins, one can write masterpieces, true masterpieces, while—and here you see what fortune hangs on—were these same tatters passed under a French dye, the most respectable manufacturers and the most influential tradesmen, men wearing the ribbon, people who have country homes at Ville-d'Avray, would not dare to place them in their shop-windows."

"Why?" Moscowitch asked.

"Because it would not be profitable."

"I believe," said Moscowitch, "that you are laughing at me now."

"Aren't you rich? Then raillery cannot touch you. In France it is impossible to laugh at riches, this impiety is forbidden by our adulatory customs. Yet, if you had talent, the common law would get possession of you: until then, be content and walk with a high head."

They entered the *Revue spéculative*. The presentation of Moscowitch caused no curiosity. Fortier was amiable and Van Baël, absent-minded. Yet when, prompted by Entragues, he declared: "I wish to regenerate the theater through pity," eyes were uplifted and Renaudeau, diverted, dragged him to the stake. It was one of the most amusing courses of dramatic history ever given for the instruction of a beginner. Renaudeau cited names that no one had ever heard of, and Moscowitch took notes, promised to read, and thanked him.

This facile irony irritated Van Baël, who with a tone of superiority took the Russian under his protection, gave him some good advice, and finally two or three quite useless letters of introduction to directors who never opened, naturally, their doors to strangers.

"Ah! here is the Marquise!" said Fortier, as a woman with an extravagant dress entered. Her temples confessed that she had passed the fortieth year. She was strapped in a black bodice studded by way of buttons with authentic old silver coins; a collar with similar medals on her neck, her curled hair, dyed a rose-colored blond, falling on her shoulders; a hat *à la Longueville* bristling with rebellious plumes; bracelets as far as her elbows under her large sleeves; a heavy furred gown, opened and thrown back, behind which the two plates of a clasp as large as two shields were suspended as far as the neck. She raised her curving nose and fixed on Fortier her impudent eyes of a woman who has thumbed, without omitting one single page, the album of lust. She spoke affectedly:

"My dear Fortier, and my *Lauzun*?"

"Madame, I should love to be yours," Fortier said.

Her eyes responded with lightning rapidity:

"I accept."

She said:

"Now, you have promised me proofs for this week."

While Fortier was trying to convince her that the *Revue spéculative* was unworthy of her qualities, that money, rare everywhere, had a sort of dread of his till, Moscowitch asked:

"Who is this woman?"

"They call her the Marquise, why I do not know. Her coins have earned her better names: the Medal Cabinet, and this one, the Reliquary, most cruel of all. Then, as she signs herself 'Françoise' to kitchen recipes, Renaudeau has nicknamed her Françoise the Blue-Stocking. She probably has a real name; it is either ordinary or insignificant."

"To think that at my age," Renaudeau said, "I have never seen any blue stockings. The *modistes* wear them red most often, and it is among them I have my loves."

"Red? I, too," the Marquise said.

She camped her foot on a chair, lifting her petticoat as far as the garter.

The leg was still pretty and her repartee clever.

Renaudeau, confessing himself outflanked by the movement, bowed and assumed the air of one wishing to say, "I regret I can do no more."

"And I, too," the eyes of the Marquise answered.

Having bowed, not without a certain ironic charm, she departed, certain now that her article would be accepted.

Fortier chided his secretary. She had paid with her person, payment signed and received. Her prose could no longer be refused; but she should get no money.

"Renaudeau, you must sacrifice yourself."

"Well," said Renaudeau, "this jade is full of surprises. I accept."

Moscowitch, very much astonished, found these customs singular. He asked Entragues:

"And will this woman's article, even if wretched, appear in the *Revue* simply because she has shown her leg?"

"Yes," Entragues answered distractedly, for he reflected, while listening to Moscowitch's question, how dangerous such a profoundly naive man might be. "He must be full of spontaneity, like a concealed spring which the blow of a pickax puts in motion. Some day Sixtine will wound his heart and violent effusions of love will burst forth from the wound. It would be well to watch him, to infuse him with literary distraction. This would be a way: have him understand that he has genius, that he owes it to himself, to his two fatherlands, to humanity, not to put the marvelous plant in jeopardy, the plant which ... which ... God, Nature, Glory and other entities ... I am not at all jealous ... my chapter cured me of jealousy this morning. I have tortured Delia Preda and the tormentor has let fall the pincers which tortured my flesh ... not jealous, but uneasy. In short, it is a question of myself, I have incorporated Sixtine into my life. If she is taken away, I am mutilated."

"Indeed," he told Moscowitch, as there entered a lean, insipid-looking person, whose eyes were terrified by apocalyptic visions, "here is a type worth observing. It is in vain for you to have talent, and even more than talent (*good*), my dear friend (*these familiar words give value to the compliment, by clothing it with sincerity*), yes, despite my inclination to irony I must end by confessing the impression you have made on me (*his eyes light up*), yes, more than talent (*the flower expands: open, precious flower of vanity, exhale thy heady odor, intoxicate him!*) ... well, nothing must be neglected ... observation ... the little characteristic facts ... these nothings which, capitalized, give a drama, just as a novel, an inimitable air of real Truth (*apostate*) ... Truth ... my dear ... the truth (*a ladder would be needed to paint on the curtain of nothingness the capital belonging to this word....*

TRUTH

He commences to understand that I wish him well) ... Listen to him, he is called Blondin and was as fine as his name, as pretty as a heart, but women have left only the shell."

"Ah! my poor friends," Blondin lamented, after having remained huddled in his chair, "there is another one this week. This makes the seventh this year, without counting all those which pass unnoticed ... Ah!"

"What is it?" Moscowitch, inquired.

"A premature burial."

"Ah! my poor friends," sighed Blondin, stretching his contracted hands towards a vision of horror, "to be buried alive, to twist in the coffin with anguish and suffocation ... and first of all the calvary of cataleptics condemned to torment ... the hypocritical tears ... the stirrings in the chamber ... the ominous carpenter ... the church ... the *Dies irae* ... the stones and the wet ground, and the rain falling, falling, falling on the oak ... then silence, silence, silence...."

"My dear Blondin," Fortier said, "you should get married. That will divert you."

"Poor woman!" Renaudeau exclaimed. "Let him rather take light o' loves."

"But I believe," Entragues said, "that his principles...."

"Yes, this unfortunate creature is truly mal-treated by life. What a specimen. And not one of us is assured against such a disorder! When one thinks of this possible end, it is best to follow Fortier's advice, marry, become bourgeois, procreate and only read the first page of the papers, the *feuilleton*, the exchange, and deny oneself all other sundry facts as too exciting."

"More than one of us will end," Entragues said, "with marriage, corporeal progeniture."

"Do you not find it odd, Entragues, that to marry, one is forced to submit to ceremonies and to the assent of one's contemporaries?"

"I imagine," Entragues said, "that a religious marriage, in a tiny solitary chapel, by an affected priest, in the presence of two or three dear friends, with no discourse other than the admirable words of the missal, without celebrations, without dances, without any consequent dinner—I believe that in such forms marriage is an interesting act which one would pleasurably recall, especially if a red lamp hung from the vault, if the priest had a fine, well-accentuated voice, and if one loved one's bride. As practiced, marriage is the most repugnant of the ceremonies imposed on men by tradition. It is, what? the official authorization given by society to a man and woman to live together. There! Ah! analysis goes to the bottom of everything, even to the most sacred customs."

Entragues was almost applauded for his phrases, spoken with a very noble conviction. It was the thought of every one present, expressed in splendid language.

David Dazin alone seemed sad. He was a lean and tall Belgian with curled hair, blond as the moon and as disquieting. His vanity was pleased by the hoaxes of the papers who jeered, from time to time, at his theory of colored vowels. Although he had taken this from Rimbaud, he imagined that he had invented it and he prided himself on being a revolutionary genius. Rimbaud was a madman with gleams which often touched on talent; Dazin was a sane man in quest of madness: it had frustrated him, for his unaccountable amputations only formed, on the clown's arena, poses that were neither new nor pleasant.

He feigned a deep grief of feelings wounded in their delicacy, and addressed Entragues:

"What, you associate with red, that is with bright coppers, such an image as a religious marriage! The organs prevail there: the tone is black."

"But," Entragues answered, "I do not fix any obligatory association. I see my sanctuary illuminated by feeble red lamp, a quite occasional and personal association. As for marriage, it is, doubtless, white, blue, rose, usually; for me it is black with a red speck and some beams of dull gold."

"That would be better," Dazin returned, "but red alone, as I understood it, would pain me."

"Ah! how sensitive this poor Dazin is?"

"Entragues," interrupted Fortier, "do you wish a box for the Odéon, tomorrow?"

"Oh! no, thanks."

"Be careful, there is a surprise. They will play...."

"What?"

"You will see! You will see!"

"Very well," said Entragues.

CHAPTER XXV

DEPARTURE

"Déjà il rêvait à une thébaïde raffinée,
à un désert confortable, à une arche immobile
et tiède où il se réfugierait loin de l'incessant
déluge de la sottise humaine."
Huysmans, *A Rebours*.

Moscowitch, feeling bored and out of place among such obscure discussions, bowed to the honorable editors, and excusing himself to Entragues, left.

"Ah!" Renaudeau said, "perhaps we are going to learn who this new manufacturer of dramatic literature is."

"I do not know myself," Entragues answered, "having brought him here only through international courtesy."

"And to get rid of him?" Fortier questioned. "But Renaudeau does not permit himself to be overreached. Besides, we shall see, for he has left me a copy: '*The Voluntary Expiation*, drama in eight scenes.' Ah! there is an *Explanatory Note*: 'In default of social justice, inner justice punishes the guilty; one has opprobrium for its end; the other, rehabilitation; the one abases, the other elevates.' A period, then a dash, and these three words twice underlined: 'VOLUNTARY EXPIATION SANCTIFIES.'"

"Well!" Entragues said, "it is quite puerile, but perhaps the text contains interesting details."

"Yes," Renaudeau put in, "a new form justifies all subjects, as a fine resilvering conceals verdigris. Do you ask for indulgence?"

"Oh! no," Entragues returned, "although I have a certain interest in having him believe he is destined for fame. If you wish to oblige me, humor him with illusions until the final dagger thrust."

"So you are becoming wicked, Entragues?" asked Fortier.

"No, it is just for the sport."

He requested an envelope and, after inserting the box ticket with his card and writing the name of Madame Sixtine Magne upon it, he had it dispatched to her. As soon as the office boy left, remorse seized him: perhaps he would have done better to go there in person. No. Yes. No. Yes.

Renaudeau, who had glanced over the manuscript, arrested this fatiguing game of see-saw by saying:

"It is not, perhaps, so bad. When a drama has a philosophy, it appears superior to anything we have. Our classical theater is so denuded of mystic sense! Corneille does politics, Racine, the psychology of the laboratory, and as for Molière, he is closed to aught that is not ruse, enjoyment, banal remarks on love, and vague statements. When he wishes to take up any traits of manners, it is to subject women to the materialism of life, to rail at nobility, because there is none, or at the doctors, because they cannot cure him of his hypochondria. Veuillot, but Hello especially, has judged him well: he shuts the door. It is really the theater of a Gassendist."

"You are speaking of Molière?" asked Calixte, entering. "He is a wretch: he has jeered at the dreamer."

"Nevertheless," objected Van Baël, "what of Alceste and Don Juan?"

"But," Renaudeau interposed, "even had he done nothing at all, he would be, like Voltaire, beyond criticism."

"Don Juan would have charm, were it not for his ridiculous rustics," Calixte said. "But see how everything shrinks in the brain of this bourgeois: if Don Juan is not a fastidious person, if in the vast field of corn he does not choose the finest, the highest and the most golden, if he makes a sheaf of everything, he is no longer Don Juan, he is a trailer after petticoats."

"Precisely," Entragues said, "but if he loves them all, it is because he idealizes them all."

"I do not think so," Calixte said. "Molière only made these countrywomen victims of Don Juan to put the comic note into his play: he had to make his audience laugh and the first conception that came was good. And Alceste? Does this person who detests men and who prefers solitude to the few concessions demanded by a pretty woman—does this man find, at the end of five acts, a single word to paint the soul-state of a hater of humanity? He is only a crabbed fellow. Above all else, he places the joy of being himself in liberty, far from the world, and he does not know how to express it: he has no soul! With what delicious grace does the so ridiculed Thisbé, the Thisbé of Théophile, tell Bersiane of her dread of noise, external life, the movement of things:

THISBE

Sais-tu pas bien que j'aime à rêver, à me taire
Et que mon naturel est un peu solitaire,
Que je cherche souvent à m'ôter hors du bruit?

Alors, pour dire vrai, je hais bien qui me suit:
Quelquefois mon chagrin trouverait importune
La conservation de la bonne fortune,
La visite d'un Dieu me désobligerait,
Un rayon de soleil parfois me fâcherait.

"And what do the professors mean by telling us that the sentiment of nature was unknown in the seventeenth century, when we find such verses, again in the same Théophile:

Les roses des rosiers, les ombres, les ruisseaux,
Le murmure des vents et le bruit des oiseaux,

or such lines:

Chaque saison donne ses fruits,
L' automne nous donne ses pommes,
L'Hyver donne ses longues nuits,
Pour un plus grand repos des hommes.
Le Printemps nous donne des fleurs,
Il donne l'âme et les couleurs
A la feuille qui semblait morte....

"I do not know the rest. One always reads the same books," Calixte concluded, "without suspecting that only those which the majority disdains have interest."

"Théophile," Entragues remarked, "is one of the rare French poets. He is full of delicate reveries. I know him well for I love him:

Prête-moi ton sein pour y boire
Des odeurs qui m' embaumeront.

"The second Théophile has spoken of him without having read him. This is obvious, for why should he have passed his time in explaining him, if he had known him? One only talks of what one does not know; to talk of what one knows seems useless; one gets bored and bores others as well. That is why criticism is, most often, so disagreeable when it is well informed, and partaking of an emetic laxity, the rest of the time."

"Like that of Bergeron," Calixte said. "Why have you accepted his dilution of nonsense on Verlaine and Huysmans?"

"As an advertisement, my dear," Fortier answered. "It is virtually printed on the blue sheets of the initial and final announcements."

"He is witty," Renaudeau said, "and that amuses: one must live. It has gained us several alleged subscriptions."

"The man is pretending," Entragues declared. "He is as incapable of feeling Verlaine's poetry as I of feeling Molière's."

"And then," Calixte interposed, "he is truly too destitute of principles. After some savage attack, he offers you, what? another article, 'this one serious, according to my real convictions.' As Goncourt says, there are 'droll vulgarians.' Ah! I see nothing since Hennequin, whose precision of method and sureness of deduction pardoned an absolutism of theory that was a little hard. I see nothing except those of to-morrow, those who still speak in the desert. It is, nevertheless, interesting to read the alleged opinion of an intelligence on works old or new...."

"There remains Fiction and Poetry," Entragues said, "and for me that suffices."

Dazin, who had only offered some inarticulations since his blue and red vowels had foundered under the gales of talk, declared:

"Nothing, nothing more, and besides, there was never anything; but one believed, and now one no longer believes. I love them. You will soon see the *Abyssales* which are now being printed: you will see. It is a chaplet of medals where, with a certain material force, I have restored the profiles of women. I believe they are in a tolerable style. Here are the first lines of the first one:

Basilisse, icon.—In the lecherous and parthenoide incognition, the abysmal gleam of the muliebrile future towards the flames and the chimerical burning ah (wings unfold for this flight and eyeballs glisten: silk rumples at the carnal rustling)! slumbers and blond the cruel senses are veiled!

She.

Here blond the gloom.

To smile at the growth of vernal grass and the gladioles died of ennui the blood returns to the heart.

Sharp already? The Arachnean dead in rents and the pungency the red and the buckler is resolved on the aureoles twinly surge the Breasts."

Among the flakes of this verbal fog, Entragues suspected Dazin of having wished to suggest the birth of puberty and the awaking of the senses. He knew the facile arcena of these strained phrases of which Dazin was not the inventor. Such a style was not absolutely to be condemned, provided one only used it for the sake of desired obscurities and with the glossary of a context.

Mortified at being understood by a simple analyst, Dazin left.

"He believes himself," Renaudeau said, "a Mallarmé or a more subtle Laforgue."

"He has not even surprised," Calixte Heliot answered, "the most elementary of their processes."

"The processes of a poet," Entragues said, "are part of his talent: it would be quite sterile to possess it. Mallarmé plays with the complementary colors of those with which he wishes to suggest vision. If Dazin had remained, I would have given him this secret and also told him that to be a more subtle Laforgue, one must have more than a capricious syntax, abusive metaphors of rare words, and the like—one must have a spontaneity which touches the heart."

Hubert and Calixte left together and walked at random through the streets, continuing, almost always in agreement, the conversation begun in the Revue.

This time, again, they did not separate until the hour of sleep; they were happy in enjoying each other, with the certainty of likewise delighting each other, of expressing concordant thoughts, of offering nothing that would be a blasphemy to the other.

As they were noting the parallelism of these two evenings which chance meetings had given them, at a short interval, Hubert remarked the duality in the development of events.

"When an act is produced, it is always produced a second time. This is an axiom. It is evident that, to demonstrate it, one would have to be fortified with a multiplicity of historic anecdotes, and I do not know if this is possible. As far as I and my past life are concerned, there is such a surprising and frightful exactitude in the axiom that I believe I could predict nearly half the things which will happen to me from to-day until the last sleep. Besides, this axiom, perhaps, is quite personal to me, special to my organism. Such a tendency to repetition is not the source of any joy. I wish that pleasures could be doubled like pains and that the proportion, in short, could remain the same, but consider the infirmity of mathematics applied to the human soul: it is assuredly less painful to me to have seven griefs for one felicity than to bear a double weight counterbalanced by such a weak duplication as that of one to two. Prolonged to infinity, the two proportions would go on eternally equipoised, but the scale of pains breaks with its chains and crushes our hearts."

At the request of Calixte, skilful in diverting a conversation headed for the abysses, Entragues related some of his plans to his friend. What works to be constructed! It was not that the freestone was lacking, nor cement, nor accessories; it was a question of time. He had, ready for erection, more ideas than a century could utilize, and sometimes the things which would never be done frightened and haunted him like a swarming of gnomes. He had thought of this on certain mornings: to put some books, his copybooks, his notes, his written sheets in a valise and hide himself for the rest of his life in a closed house, facing the sea. He saw it built on the dunes, between the strand and the first trees of the coast: no vegetation nearby excepting the pallid grass, the violet thistles and the tall darnels; the view of steeples far off, on the land side; on the other side, the sea and a lighthouse, amid wind and wave, like a symbol. Wagons pass, full of sea-weed; horses and men pant on the sand, yoked to the labor of the fecundation of the ground, and he, yoked to the labor of the sterilization of desires, would watch them pass. Towards the equinoxes, the spray of waves agitated by moon and tempest would come to strike against his window, like a bird's wing. And birds would also come towards the gleam of his lamp and he would open his window to the spray of waves and the wings of birds. Like a monster, he would be alone. "For we are monsters, my poor Calixte, we have put our duty above life; our souls afar from men, like fabulous dragons, we guard imaginary treasures, and we know it, and to this nothingness we sacrifice all, even our life! We have hearts of anchorites and we would court women! Ah! were I there—a hermit among my dreams, an excellent shelter—I should write what I shall perhaps not write: a work. But to what end? Now, at other times I would like to get into some fixed habit, punctually deliver myself to love, quarrel with my wife at stated hours, rise late, enfeeble the ennui of evenings in the vain noise of theaters, eat nourishing foods which charge the nerves with vibrant fluids, and busy myself, during rainy hours, with an honorable compilation."

"It would be better to clothe oneself in love," Calixte said. "To transfer one's egoism to a woman: to be jealous of one's own joys more than of hers, in fine, to give to another the absurd happiness one would not wish for oneself; to dream that she is happy, that she feels it and knows it is through my agency."

"Do you imagine that this would be possible for us?" Entragues asked.

He made no allusion to his personal sentiments, for even Calixte was not his confidant. In questioning his friend or in answering him, he spoke with full liberty, completely abstract.

"Yes," Calixte answered, "the 'Imitation' gives the clue. It suffices to transfer to a creature the love, proportionately lessened, which the priest feels towards God. It would be a sort of obligation to love which one would impose upon oneself, the first rule of a more general rule of life, freely and Chistianly accepted, once for all."

"I had not thought of this," Entragues said, "of love considered as a spiritual discipline."

"Such is the exact formula," Calixte declared. "If we can yet save ourselves, we and all similar monsters, it is through Christianity and Christian discipline. This will singularly elevate our souls and it may curb our transcendental egoisms!"

"We should require Beatrices," Hubert said.

"They can be created," Calixte responded, "and we can baptize a nobly profiled woman with divine love."

(Hubert received this note on the following day:

"It is perhaps quite compromising, but I am free. Be good enough to call for me at eight o'clock."

Then he began to dream of the joy of shared pleasures, and instantly the fourth chapter of *The Adorer* found itself shaped.)

CHAPTER XXVI

THE ADORER
IV. The Blond Forest

"Nous promenions notre visage
(Nous fûmes deux, je le maintiens)
Sur maints charmes de paysage,
O soeur, y comparant les tiens."
Stéphane Mallarmé.
Prose pour des Esseintes.

The blond forest is filled with love: after the fall of sunlight and the night, smiling jewels.

"Together, our souls thrilled at the return of the primordial splendor; noons have not blinded us, for we have slept, during the heat of the day, in the shadow of our love: our tendernesses, like wings, fanned us and the freshness of our breath vaporized the perfumes.

"Like us, the forest filled with love has slept, for it is in our souls that its verdures have arisen, its birds, its drooping branches, its flowers, its murmurings and the dominating heights of its radiant trees.

"The blond forest is a body filled with love: it sleeps but sparingly and during our sleep, slumbering it sang, its body filled with love, and we heard the song of the blond forest:

Je suis le corps tout plein d'amour d'une amoureuse,
Mes herbes sont les cils trempés de larmes claires
Et mes blancs liserons sont les écrins, paupières
Où les bourraches bleues, ces yeux fleuris, reposent
Leurs éclatants saphirs, étoilés de sourires,
Je suis le corps tout plein d' amour d'une amoureuse.

Je suis le corps tout plein d'amour d'une amoureuse.
Mes lierres sont les lourds cheveux et mes viournes
Contournent leurs ourlets, pareils à des oreilles.
O muguets, blanches dents! Eglantines, narines!
O gentianes roses, plus roses que les lèvres!
Je suis le corps tout plein d'amour d'une amoureuse,

Je suis le corps tout plein d'amour d'une amoureuse.

Mes saules out le profil des tombantes épaules,
Mes trembles sont des bras tremblants de convoitise,
Mes digitales sont les doigts frêles, et les oves
Des ongles sont moins fins que la fleur de mes mauves,
Je suis le corps tout plein d'amour d'une amoureuse,

Je suis le corps tout plein d'amour d'une amoureuse.
Mes sveltes peupliers out des des tailles flexibles,
Mes hêtres blancs et durs sont de fermes poitrines
Et mes larges platanes courbent comme des ventres
L'orgueilleux bouclier de leurs écorces fauves,
Je suis le corps tout plein d'amour d'une amoureuse,

Je suis le corps tout plein d'amour d'une amoureuse.
Boutons rouges, boutons sanglants des paquerettes,
Vous êtes les fleurons purs et vierges des mamelles,
Anémones, nombrils! Pommeroles, auréoles!
Mûres, grains de beauté! Jacinthes, azur des veines!
Je suis le corps tout plein d'amour d'une amoureuse,

Je suis le corps tout plein d'amour d'une amoureuse.
Mes ormes sont la grâce des reins creux et des hanches,
Mes jeunes chênes, la force et le charme des jambes,
Le pied mi de mes aunes se cambre dans les sources
Et j'ai des mousses blondes, des mystères, des ombres,
Je suis le corps tout plein d'amour d'une amoureuse!

"When we had heard the love song of the blond forest, we awoke, and together we enjoyed the blue calm of the last hours.

"The beloved madonna gave me a last smile, night separated us and, left alone, I dreamed of the delights of shared love."

CHAPTER XXVII

THE EDUCATION OF MAIDENS

"Enamourée, tant que mon coeur étouffe!"
Ciacco Dell' Anguillara.

Scraps of conversation of the preceding evening returned to his memory after he left. The approaching pleasure of the promised evening led his thoughts to the theater, and he mentally re-read some of the dramatic projects he had conceived and written.

Two or three particularly interested him. They sketched some brief scenes of stupidity, egoism, ill-nature, the eternal and contemporary eagerness to engage with the passion embedded in very young hearts. He merely showed simple persons dominated by a vice, an ambition, a mania; no analysis except in the rough; probabilities carefully extracted from the improbable confusion of ordinary life; soul states which tend to become symbolic; no mere news, no sudden changes, no modification of facts. What an agreeable spectacle, for example, in the legend of the Prodigal Son, defined in images, or the story which a biscuit manufacturer prints on rough pale rose paper for his trade, or some popular tale, or higher, among holy or saintly things, Passion, the Life of the Magdalene, a narrative dramatized by a little of the unforeseen struggles of spirit against flesh. Everything came back to that.

Prey to a devouring intellectual excitement, Hubert walked rapidly with no destination in mind beyond the desire to free himself by means of the natural denouements of the agitated world which stirred in him, assailing, like grapeshot of besiegers, the fortress of his logic.

Finally, as he was walking along the rue des Tuileries, near the wooden and zinc booth where at certain times people exhibit paintings, and where at other times young girls exhibit their capacities as teachers; near this booth, the enchanted army disappeared, returning to limbo.

The booth was shut and the street empty, but Entragues saw the door open and the highway as far as the garden fill with little pupils, with mammas hanging to their coats, proudly, and black paper-boxes under their arms, faded complexions, breasts drooping through the constant bending of the chest, ugly robes without even the coquetry of a beggar's colored rags, ink-stained fingers, sleeves made glossy by rubbing against wooden tables, and orthographic preoccupations in the eyes of those at the age of a mild little love affair with "the friend of my brother" or "the brother of my girl friend."

He distinguished, however, a future woman between two who wore spectacles. She walked with a sprightly and decided air, carrying her body that was rebellious to the obligatory deformations; she was brunette and garbed in a becoming black. A young man, who moved timidly among all these skirts, lifted his hat as he glanced at her; she answered with a little motion of the head, joined him without shame and both, arms united, departed. In the middle of the street, she threw over the wooden fence her black box, inkstand, pencils, penholder and papers; these articles the wind blew about; the girl joyously clapped her hands, seemed to pause for a long breath; then they fled. They hastened with reason, for a teacher, warned, was running towards her pupil, the hope of her cage and the honor of her manger; they hastened with reason: for they were going to live.

Entragues understood quite well what had happened. It was during the dictation that a sudden lance thrust had pierced her heart, making a breech in the breastplate of boards. Blood had rushed, mingling with rules of syntax: she was saved!

Entragues was not at all satisfied with the too humorously ironic form which the anecdote took. He decided, in case he ever returned to it with a view of writing, to introduce a more methodical and haughty protestation. The instruction given to young girls did not vex him, but its quality did: they were crammed, like Turkish women, with maize-flour, so as to obtain a forced corpulency, although fine dieting is necessary for those creatures who can so easily be deformed. Neither grammar, nor geography, nor distasteful chronological history, nor practically anything now customary was suitable for women, but only the Old and New Testament, the Life of the Saints, solid mystic readings, then the poets, the romancers of dreams, all that can, in gloomy hours, reflower in the soul, at the call of holy harps, at the summons of kisses of love, under children's caresses.

These thoughts accompanied him as far as his home, whither the rain forced him to return.

He had not wished to think directly of Sixtine all day, for fear of withering the expected pleasures by a precocious plucking; she had her revenge; although it was long before the hour of the rendezvous, he held her before his eyes, but changing and retreating, like a woman who comes and goes, busied with her toilet, disappearing all white, reappearing clothed in color, a summer landscape whose nuances obey the transparent play of clouds.

CHAPTER XXVIII

THE ESTHETIC THRILL

"Le style est inviolable."
Ernest Hello.

"Besides, here is the spring, it will enliven me. You will see," said the actor, with a malicious smile. "You will see. I do not detest the country, once in a while. It inspires fresh ideas that sometimes are lucrative. It is like the theater...."

"The public seems uneasy," said Sixtine. "One would swear that it does not understand."

"While waiting to be shocked. It is permissible to curse gold, not to scorn it. Would you," continued Hubert, "incite men to the mockery of the secret quintessence of their ideal? To scoff at lucre in the theater is to blaspheme God in a church."

"Oh! my manner, Monsieur," said the actress, "never signifies anything...."

This was taken by Sixtine almost as a personal allusion. She would have liked to hear herself addressed in a phrase which permitted such a reply. All the hypocrisy imposed on women protected in syllables against the stupidity of men who never guess. When she heard:

"... Yes ... I believe you have some illusions concerning my true nature...."

Her hands came together in a gesture of applause. She, too, was misunderstood; she felt herself capable of using a similar phrase. The audience murmured.

"You are mistaken," she told Hubert. "Here is sympathy, if these sounds are, as I believe, a mark of indignation against the impudent foolishness of this man."

"I think," said Hubert, "that they are growing angry against the boldness of the woman. Visibly before them, she lies to her duty which is to lie and go noiselessly about her love affairs."

"... Be honest and rich, the rest is vanity...."

"There is an unbending," remarked Hubert. "This last has been received as a flattery. They now believe she is going to reproach him because she has only been honest and rich, thanks to herself. There! that's right. This is fine, this is invigorating! Ah! ah!"

"I told you of admirable things of the earth, I told you of the true reality, that which you must choose...."

"Sixtine leaned forward, drawn by the magnetism of the noble speech, then fell back in her seat, dreamy, her fingers trembling, feeling the imperious desire of a hand to envelop her hand. Without moving her head, she turned her eyes towards Hubert: he was listening, less moved than fascinated.

"I want to live! Do you understand, madman that you are!... I thirst after serious things! I want to breathe the full air of the sky!"

The same esthetic thrill shook them at the same instant: their breath came faster, they had grown pale; their lips opened as for silent exclamations.

The electric current which descended down their spines with rapid waves stirred their limb, and at last, unconsciously attracted to each other, they were forced to let their hands obey the attraction of the fluids.

Then, the intensity of the emotional excitement doubled: their beings floated in a warm and caressing eddy, under the delicious downpour of a water-fall warmed by a mysterious sun, and the corporeal flowers of sensuality burned to open.

They listened, without letting a syllable of the magic prose escape their ears, and they dreamed while listening; they forgot "the omnipotence of inferior minds;" they deified each other, they ascended, supple and light, the mystic steps, summoned now by the illusion of a very pure and very expanding air at the summit of a narrow mountain above the clouds. Indeed, they had, "agitated minds," as the male character of the piece had so well said; they said to the whole world: "Your joys are not my joys;" all that stirred outside of them, all things that agitated below their flight were quite truly "infantile and noxious," in the silence they were in rapport with their "old friend"; they cried aloud to life: "It is no longer a question of all this! Adieu!..."

And at the end, when they went down with the curtain's fall to the stupefied room, the same stifled cry issued from their mouths, the cry of Hamlet:

"Horrible! Horrible! Horrible!"

Entragues, swept away by a movement of anger, so little in accord with his usual character, thus challenged a man who was hissing:

"Monsieur, you are a cur!"

As the rascal contented himself with shrugging his shoulders, in this way taking his key away, Entragues felt sadness and shame welling within him in place of anger.

"We will protest," said Sixtine, "by foregoing the rest of the play."

It was nine o'clock. Some persons, having been spared the rise of the curtain, were strolling under the Odéon galleries, looking at the latest novels: Hubert recognized several eminent critics and thought he could read, underneath the ribbon of their hats, the repetition of the naive avowal Collé made in his *Journal*: "I undertake to criticize plays because I cannot write any myself." They spoke of the revival of the little *machine*, and one of them deemed, in a simple and new style, that "the need of it did not perhaps make itself very acutely perceived." This irony was relished.

"We shall go on foot," said Sixtine.

The weather was humid, but mild. They walked through little dark streets, grazed by occasional passersby, in silence.

She asked him if he personally knew the author of this piece so unlike the things ordinarily heard at the theater.

"He is dead," said Hubert. "He was the noblest writer of our time."

Half of the young writers recognized him as their master and almost all had been touched by his influence. In his works were pages of an incomparable magnificence and purity of language. He truly gave the impression of the two souls of Goethe and Edgar Allen Poe melted into one and lodged in the same person.

Sixtine was surprised that he was not better known, but Hubert assured her that he was known to those who could understand him. Others would only be capable of acquiring the verbal knowledge of his name, and to what end? He proceeded just like some other contemporaries whom Hubert named, but when the thieves of glory would have used up their life-interest, the others would enter the house, the parchment of immortality in their hands, and would expel the intruders. Perhaps at this very hour still others, more unknown, were lying in a cellar or were dying bedridden, whose names would to-morrow fill the world with an unexpected gleam.

"Well! Madame, think that Jesus, who was the son of God and whose works and speech, sown in time and space, have yielded great harvests, think that Jesus died so unknown that Josephus, almost his contemporary, the grandson of the high-priests and descendant of the Maccabees, captain general of the Galileans, historian of all the little details of Jewish history,— Josephus had never heard of Jesus. I could give you more accessible examples, but this is primordial and those among us, who go through with an obscure life, unjustly, should not deem themselves humiliated: their day will come if they are worthy, and if not, it is quite useless that a light should spring up which will have to be extinguished."

"You are all quite haughty," said Sixtine, "you would not be vexed to be compared, in your wretched distresses, with the Son of Man."

"Oh!" answered Hubert, "I never dreamed of such a ridiculous blasphemy. Just as saints and less lofty souls, endowed with good will, take for example the human career of Jesus, and console themselves for their merited sufferings by thinking of the unmerited injuries of Christ, so it is permitted us to assuage the feeling of our disappointments by similar meditations. Would you have us take for themes of prayer the life of Socrates, who died unknown to the Greeks? Would you have us take Spinoza? He was a polisher of spectacle glasses, a drinker of milk, and he died of starvation, not of penury, because his mind was distracted and he forgot to nourish himself, having other things to do."

Sixtine was confounded with astonishment that he should give her such barren talk after their mutual esthetic and sentimental emotions. She attempted to reascend to the source to see if, this time, the craft would not take another branch of the stream.

She spoke of the acting, which she found perfect.

"Alas!" said Hubert. "Ignorance, sometimes, resembles genius among actors. Whoever is ignorant and yet must get out of a difficulty, invents badly or well, has recourse to personal souvenirs, to intuitive gestures. No, those we heard are perfect: they know all they have learned. Especially, nothing unforeseen: the foot goes like this, the hand like that, etc."

"At least," said Sixtine, "they pronounce well and speak clearly."

"It is proper, but without conviction. What woman, besides, outside of two or three select creatures...."

"I," thought Sixtine, "I, for example."

"... Could take this rôle royally enough to make one feel that it is not a rôle? Oh! the public is not exacting. The women come here to distract themselves, the men because it gives them ideas after a good dinner. Pathetic things to the former, cantharides to the latter. If they followed their inclinations most women would go to the Eden and most men to the Ambigu."

"I owe you," said Sixtine, "a very noble pleasure and I am grateful. We are at my door."

Hubert, recognizing the door, had a vision of lost time; he uttered a word which atoned somewhat for his awkward digressions:

"Already!"

"If it were not so late, I should have offered you a cup of tea, ten minutes by the fire-place which awaits me, but really...."

"Oh! I entreat you!"

"It is because ... no, it is not possible."

"In that case, you should not have made me think of it," said Hubert in a tone of chagrin.

"You had not thought of it? Then, go back to the very place where you did not think of it, and you will return in peace."

"Five minutes, only five minutes!"

"Be sensible, I will look for you to-morrow."

"Only as far as your door!"

"For what reason, then? Come, ring for me, if you please."

He obeyed. The door opened, she offered him her hand, then slowly, with movements of weariness or regret, she crossed the threshold. Still more slowly she pushed the door behind her, pausing twice before closing it.

At the moment of the inexorable sound, Hubert experienced a great sadness. He remained there for a few seconds, without thought, then suddenly a quite illogical association of ideas made him see once more the quasi-nuptial room of the "dark Marceline," and in this story he now divined, without really knowing why, premonitory ironies. Then he walked away, dreaming of doors which close, of doors which have been opened and which no longer open.

CHAPTER XXIX

PANTOMIME

"Il paraît que l'opéra était fini."
E. and J. de Goncourt,
Idées et Sensations.

Entragues, endowed with a deductive mind, liked to find his bearings—to know what he was about. To recall the past, confront it with the present, determine the resultant of the two terms, the future—this he called living. Nothing, in fact, clarifies the conscious mind more than these analytical processes. What a philter! The state of one's soul is clearly perceived. It is an egoistic enjoyment, but as salubrious as opening the windows after awaking in the morning.

He saw the cold gardens, the trees despoiled of their illusions: could he, with a glance, warm the earth again and bedeck the trees?

No, he only acquired the certainty of his impotence, an immense acquisition.

"With a glance? There certainly is a certain way of looking at things which makes them tremble like conquests under the conqueror's eyes. The book of universal magic should teach this. Satan knows it. But Faust is in hell. That denouement was a good lesson: we will not be caught again! Now, what is momentary love at the cost of eternal life?

"I must confess that I was deliciously agitated yesterday. But why? I realize it now, though I did not yesterday. Yesterday I revelled in perfect unselfconsciousness: I had to leave the flower-bed in order to breathe the perfume of flowers.

"It is true that I had breathed them in advance. Ah! I remember it all. It was not a flower-bed, but a forest,—it comes to the same thing: one can take the wrong symbol.

"So, there is no present. My calculations are simplified. The future is uncertain, for, thinking that I was penetrating the jungle of a somewhat disordered forest, I found myself in the smooth walks of a pretty little parterre: we were very well-behaved there, we did not trample on the flower-beds with heedless feet, and we breathed the fragrance of the flowers with fitting gestures of assent. Thus only the past has some chances of existence.

"Here is the question reduced to the simplest unity: is it worth while traveling for the sake of memories? All who have gone to Constantinople or to the Gobelins can respond.

"But to live again, one must have lived.

"Is it I who have spoken? I thought I heard an oracular voice.

"No matter, the premise of my logic was false, for the conclusion is absurd.

"We live in imaginary realms, that is to say in the transcendental or supernatural reality; then why not place both feet on the same plane? To dream of love, must I have pressed against my flesh the flesh of my beloved? Naïveté. Did Guido touch his madonna? It she a woman he has possessed— or only played with? For its is a true pleasure of love to reinvolve its illusory carnality in order to love, in the person of the woman, the intangible creature of one's dreams!

"I reason well, decidedly. I am a logician.

"I should have followed this career.... Ah! here is the house! Already? The same exclamation as yesterday evening! I do not get bored with myself. No, and here I am returned to the place I left."

Entragues shrugged his shoulders, thinking: "One would say that above is someone who is stronger and who mocks at us."

Then, he rang.

She was tired, pale despite the red of her robe, reclining in a large arm-chair, barricaded with cushions, very near a big wood fire; she was reading, her head thrown back.

The light, feeble and bluish, fell from a suspended lamp. Hubert suspected that she could not decipher the printed pages and thought she had assumed an attitude, but he was mistaken: Sixtine, like many women, had the eyes of a cat; she was very seriously reading *les Victimes d'Amour*.

Seeing this title on the rose-colored cover of the volume which Sixtine had thrown on the ground at his approach, Hubert had a moment of anguish.

"I misunderstood the woman!"

It seemed to him that his love was rendered abject in promiscuity with the banal adventures in this head, which nevertheless was charming and delicate under this fawn-colored hair.

"So these are the things she loves!"

"Are you annoyed?" she asked.

"Yes," Hubert answered frankly, and to get a reassuring answer, "it is because I see you taking pleasure in unworthy books."

"But I swear to you that this book is agreeable and most exciting. It pleases me, as you say, and indeed! it would be very painful to me had I mislaid the other books. I thought I had, at first: thank Heaven, the anguish was brief. Here they are," she added, searching among the cushions, "and I am sorry that there are only three of them and that I shall be obliged, after finishing them, to commence some other story again. Oh! for this sort of distraction, the quality of literature is quite indifferent to me: all I ask is that it be complicated, threatening, as absurd as impossible. It is my opium, or, if you wish, my supply of cigars. In what would you really have me interested, in your analytical things and ... what? symbolical things?"

"But yesterday?" hazarded Hubert.

"Yesterday, the esthetic emotion was presentable. It harmonized with the nuance of my robe and the form of my bodice, to which, moreover, you paid no attention."

"I beg your pardon! the shade was light green and the form was that of Brittany. You looked like a severe lady of yore confining in a rigid corselet breasts that have been mortified by penitence."

"Yes, but you acted as if I were incorporeal and only garbed with the charms of my virtues. I warn you, Monsieur, that on any future occasion when I walk with you (quite improbable occasion!), I will put on the severest black of the severest woolen robe I have."

She continued, after listlessly stirring the embers in the grate.

"The pleasure in pretty robes is quite ended. I would like a uniformed costume like nuns, not too unbecoming, so as not to weary my eyes in mirrors."

"Black," said Hubert, "would be agreeable, but why this renunciation?"

"So that the external gayety might not make a false contrast with the darkness of my soul ... I should not have received you this evening, for I am sad and forlorn."

"You promised."

"That is no reason. I have had more important promises made to me which were never fulfilled. I bear no malice, only regret."

"Let me love you?"

"And to what purpose?" asked Sixtine, drawing herself up in her chair as if stupefied.

"It will perhaps console you."

"Oh! my dear, do what you wish, I am patient and passive, but I warn you, it will be the worse for you."

"You are so discouraging!" Hubert gently returned. "Thus, you should have let me enter with you yesterday evening...."

"Did I forbid you?"

"You refused to let me."

She shrugged her shoulders.

"Did I forbid you to take hold of the door when I was closing it? Did I forbid you to ring if the first stratagem did not succeed? Did I forbid you to hasten after me while I slowly climbed the steps?... Yesterday, it was necessary to enter, and to-day it is necessary to leave ... because," she quickly added, "I am ill and inclined to go to bed. It is not an idealistic sight, I do not invite you to it. Your modesty would suffer, and mine perhaps. *A bientôt*, come again, do not fail to come again."

Without answering such impertinences, Hubert arose and violently imprisoned her in his two arms. She closed her eyes, he kissed them; he kissed her mouth; Sixtine, with a sudden start, half lifted herself, then they fall back against the cushions, interlaced. There, profiting by the fact that one of his arms relaxed its hold to travel along the body towards the bottom of the robe, she freed herself entirely (it is the moment when complicity is necessary), and standing, with crossed arms, she ironically regarded Hubert who was still on his knees.

This time it was she who walked towards him.

She took his hand, led him under the little suspended lamp and silently pointed with her finger to two or three significant red spots that were swelling at the corner of her mouth.

"Do not say a word, please, but go. It is perhaps a pity ... but I have no heart for love this evening.... You should have perceived it, my dear, if only by the color of my voice...."

CHAPTER XXX

THE MAN AND THE PRETTY BEAST

"E parvemi mirabil vanitate
Fermar in cose il cor, ch' el tempo preme,
Che mentre più le stringe, son passate."
Petrarque, *Triumph of Time.*

That evening, Hubert had had the courage to return to his home, to undress, to go to bed, to fall asleep, without admitting the intrusion, in his consciousness, of any thought. He was like a beaten dog filled with an irrational shame, and buried under the heavy covers, his eyes shut, he had attained sleep by a system of long and slow inhalings which, regulating the heart movement, calmed, then enfeebled the brain, like chloral.

In the morning, his adventure brought a smile to his face, and he even composed, in a tone of sad raillery, a series of little acrobatic verses, entitled: *The Thread*. Of fifteen stanzas, two amused him. He wrote them:

De quoi s'agit-il?
De presque rien. Ah!
Le plaisir tient a
Un fil.

C est un fil de tulle,
C'est un fil de soie:
S'en va, comme bulle,
La joie.

Then he attempted, while stirring the fire, which a moist wind was troubling, to recite to himself the sonnet of his friend, Calixte:

Les Désirs, s' envolant sur le dos des Chimères,
Jouent avec la lumière et le crin des crinères....

But his stubborn memory gave him only these two lines. He recalled that Delphin was going to put it to music, was even going to do some instrumentation on the theme as a gloss. But Delphin, for want of a fitting medium between the brass instruments and the strings, did not yet compose: he was waiting.

"In fine," thought Hubert, "I must admit that I have missed being happy. To surprise a woman, hypnotize her with kisses, chloroform her with caresses, then be united with her through the falling of cushions, with, before one's eyes, the future boredom of partial repetitions of a similar proceeding—this is called being happy!"

Heliot had related to him that once, in a similar situation, the maid had discreetly entered at the most interesting passage, asking, through the open door: "Does Madace wish her slippers?"

"Consequently, I have missed being happy once more, for such felicities are not unknown to me: it is only the color of garters that differs. Well, till tomorrow or the day after tomorrow: Sixtine is in my power. It is certainly pleasant, very pleasant.

"We will enjoy charming evenings. She is intelligent and I shall read her my manuscripts: here and there, I need a woman's opinion. It is astonishing that heretofore this has not troubled me more. When shall I see her again. To-day? No. To-morrow? No. But shall I write to her? Twice daily. She will answer in little brief and impersonal phrases, with shafts of raillery. I shall let her rail at me: I can do it, for I am sure of my case. Well, Tuesday? We shall see. Happiness leaves me cold and its regular perspectives sadden me. Thus, I, too, have pursued the pretty beast and I am satisfied. With what? With having put my foot on its shadow."

MAN AND THE PRETTY BEAST

The road, under the sun, lies, white and dusty, lies under the sun.

The pretty beast, what is it like? It runs too swiftly, one sees it run, one does not see it, the pretty beast.

The man is naked, panting and with cruel eyes, like a hunter, naked, however, and disarmed.

"Pretty beast, I would trap thee, ah I pretty beast, I have thee, pretty beast."

The man has bounded, he has put his foot on the pretty beast, his bare foot, very gently, so as not to hurt it.

"Ah! I have thee, pretty beast!"

"No, no, thou dost not have me. Thy bare foot is resting on my shadow."

"Ah! this time, pretty beast, thou art my prisoner; I have thee, pretty beast, I have thee in my hands."

"Thou hast me and thou seest me not, for the odor of my body blinds men. Thou hast me, and see!"

"See, I escape thee and I run. Run after me, run after the pretty beast."

"Ah! I am weary with running for sixty years; come, my son, it is thou who will catch the pretty beast.

"I am weary, I sit down to rest; go, it is now thy hour to run after the pretty beast!"

Having finished this rhapsody, Entragues wrote the beginning of the story of Gaetan Solange, which had long tormented him.

It was a way of explaining himself by means of an anticipated commentary, for he was on the verge, doubtless! of a similar state of soul: would not Hubert and Gaetan be true counterparts, to-morrow, if this continued?

CHAPTER XXXI

THE INFAMY OF BEING HAPPY

"I now see *distinctly*," he said, "what
manner of people these maskers are."
Poe: *Hop-Frog*

Solange's pessimism was practical: he perseveringly endeavored to make his life wretched by all sorts of very simple, yet ingenious combinations.

First of all, principles: Men lie and women deceive. There are but two motives to human acts—lucre and lust. All women with pleasant faces conceal objectionable defects. Men who are not wicked are stupid.

Other principles: All food is tainted or adulterated; it is useless to seek anything better than the bad. All streets are hideous, full of vile women, rubbish, drains and filth. All apartments lack air and light. And so on.

Consequently, and as he could not take pleasure in principles, Gaetan Solange had taken lodgings in a foul quarter, at the end of a damp court, in two or three little dark rooms. They were the most agreeable rooms he could find after years of patient search.

When he returned to his rooms, in the evening, it was amid the repugnant attacks of an army of wretched women; and sometimes a drunken vagrant barred his way through the narrow alley with insults and threats. Solange was satisfied, for this proved that the police were lax, that nobody could return to his dwelling after ten o'clock without risking his life.

A spongy cutlet, a woody cigar, bitter beer, a spotted table-cloth gave his visible satisfaction. It was thus: "What would you? If you wish to live, you must accept the inconveniences of life."

He liked to be plagued by a woman who, penniless, became refractory to all caresses—as in *Un Dilemme*—and the friends who had abused his confidence, wittingly ill-placed, were dear to him as the orthographic faults of a literary master: this proved once more the absolute rules of his grammar.

He only read newspapers, and the vilest of them, so that nothing might disturb his belief that no one wrote save to earn money, and that the viler and more lying any literature is, the more it entertains the public—all the public.

Entragues paused in his work and reflected: "We are almost in accord, yes, for if I detest to lull myself in joy and in the contentment of my heart, it is not through a desired and coddled impotence. I do not disdain life, I have never disowned its pleasures. It is neither bad nor good, it is indifferent, it is the conditional state of dreams, and that is all. To demand of life a little happiness is to give too much importance to the mechanism of the senses and to make oneself conform with corporeal invitations and with the rules of matter, whereas the will should aim towards emancipation.

"But I know the perils of asceticism and its infamies; and were I happy, I would experience astonishment rather than shame. I have never believed that this was written in my destiny. This attitude is proper, for I cannot, like a fool, believe that "this was due me," and despite some gleams of Christian humility, my pride is so superb that I cannot for any length of time admit the frailty of my merits. No person, doubtless, was ever worthy of happiness; but unless I am a Pharisee, I should not deem myself below average humanity: such a posture of kneeling would partake of weakness and cowardice. It is permitted me, without any disturbing in the order of my essential idealism, to moisten my lips from the cup which this charming woman offers me; then I shall make her drink it; then, emboldened, we shall quench our thirsts together, inhaling, like harvesters leaning over the clear spring, the delights of cooling refreshments.

"I leave to Solange his shame; he is a madman whose crippled understanding is blind to this idea: that only those who suffer from the refinements of their sensitiveness are permitted to toy ironically with the cankers that life is soiled with, and not those who delight in breathing, without disgust, the sordid purulence."

He continued to muse, without writing:

"Solange is a rather good fellow although a little uncultured, with coarse clothes and ugly shoes. At a marriage which he was obliged to attend, he met a young girl who fell in love with him, discreetly and with reserve, but seriously. She watched him, blushing under his glance in quest of defects; she lowered her eyes. When she passed near him she felt a strange fear come over her—the fear of being arrested by his arm and the fear of a banal bow. Naturally the young girl's mother introduced Solange to her; he was asked some favor, a very skillful maternal snare, since he would have to bring the information in a short while. He came, he returned, ever drawn by adroit combinations; finally, he returned for his own pleasure and found himself enmeshed before he had time to reflect. Besides, he thought of nothing, he let himself go, conquered and captive.

"They were married. Their moderate fortunes joined together became, in the hands of the intelligent young woman, a source of honest and almost luxurious comfort. Their apartment was large, light and sunny, the food carefully chosen; and instead of looking forward to the ennui of a lonely single bed, he enjoyed the constant presence of a beloved being who tinted with rose and blue the hours formerly gloomy with lonely awakenings.

"He no longer had time to scorn men or to relish their low greediness; pleasure of love, enjoyed in full naïveté, evoked no lewd images in his desires, no horror of self or of others; what others?

"In fine, he was happy!

"Happy! He! He the stubborn pessimist, he whose aversion to every ideal had astonished the most impotent! Happy! what a shame! He plunged to the depths of the abyss in which this adventure had overwhelmed his principles; he brought them back one by one; ah! they were rotting; all was ended and with them all joy of living—for he had just understood how much the wretchedness of a mediocre existence, how much the sentiment of the universal dunghill, was necessary to his happiness!"

CHAPTER XXXII

INTOXICATION

"Ὡς ἦν ἐν ἀϱχῆ"
Greek Liturgy.
"Man, meditate on the syllable Om."
The Khandogya Upanishad.

Hubert wrote two notes, and the evening of the second day knocked at Sixtine's door. Absence. A third note and another visit were likewise in vain.

"She is sulking," he thought. "So much the better. Her anger will exhaust itself against my shadow and, when she condescends to receive me, her beautiful face will be free of all vexation."

He was too assured of virtual possession even to suppose an attempt to fly from his hands. By imaginary advances, realized in desire, the union was established for ever. All scorn was impossible: she had breathed the fragrance of the philter.

Far from grieving, he congratulated himself; far from languishing, he breathed more deeply the invigorating breezes of certitude. Having achieved peace with himself, having thrown his pride overboard, his lightened bark now moving spiritedly towards the haven of golden sands, he would enter at the propitious hour.

The morning of the fourth day, he received news in this form:

"Please do not forget the soirée of the Countess on Wednesday next. This on her behalf.

"On my own behalf, I am sorry for having been too unwell and too busy either to receive you or to reply.

"But have we not eternity? S. M."

Entragues saw no disquieting bitterness in this raillery—and another day passed.

"The catalogue of obscene joys is brief, but it suffices, on certain days, to give the desire of purifying oneself for this world and the other. Solange had some rather just views before his malady: it is distressing that the chastity of devotees should be defiled in the hour when they regain their solitary oratories. I shall do well to read Tertullian and some consoling pages before retiring, for I fear the power of words. No, I shall dream of Sixtine. Dear creature of my desire, I trust in your magic: what wanton importunities will not yield to the grace of your gestures? Abode of my will, retreat of my illusions of love, appear to me and protect me!"

They were standing, interlaced. She kissed him lightly and repeatedly on the corner of his eyes, while having him breathe a rose. It could not last, he was becoming too languid.

Silvery moonlight, clouds, strident peals which usher in lightning, silvery moonlight.

The storm hovers in the velvety sky, the turbulent clouds pass, rifts pour out silvery moonlight.

It has thundered, indeed. Far away it rumbles, it rumbles! Another flash! Ah! it lightens, long! Again! He is dead.

Hubert awoke, roused by the terrible rumbling.

"Ah! Desecration! It was Sixtine. Ah! the plague of imbecile nerves!"

All during the storm, he remained up in his bed, haggard and shivering. The confusion of his sensations stunned him: he could not understand how this carnal hallucination had developed parallel with the beginning of the storm in a moonlight night. At last, when the dream's absurdity was evident to him, he grew calm and, benumbed by the cold, fell again between his covers.

"This day will be horrible. After all, it is worse than Guido, worse than Valentine! Such a retrogression is degrading. And I think I am master of myself, master of the external world, master of this universe—a woman—when I cannot even regulate the order the logical sequence of my impressions! The human mechanism should be known to me, and if consequences are unconquerable, at least the causes should submit to my will. The saints, with the aid of God, had this power; but God has deserted us and because of the modern Celsus' has left us, without bucklers, exposed to the arrows of Sin. Henceforth, all hours are its hour and we all belong to it: it has conquered time, space and number."

Hubert had never felt, as in those moments, the misfortune of being a man and of being nothing else. His pride, ruined by his passion, collapsed like an old wall, and, lying on the ruins bemoaned himself. This attraction, reasoned and combatted with the logical weapons of his character, became the stronger, dominated him consciously and unconsciously. He had come to a state where he no longer thought; his mind no longer functioned save in brief deductions, and the need of security distracted him from exact observation. During those decisive days, in which Sixtine had taken a part, without a doubt, he limited his tactics to brief recalls of presence, instead of obtruding himself point-blank and barring the road to every other unforeseen arrival.

It was easy to avoid the nocturnal visitation, by going himself to the fair visitor: if a magnetic and super-reasonable force had thrust Sixtine in his arms while asleep, this same force, according to the most elementary directions, had, on occasion, very, surely joined their realities, as it had joined their phantasms. He lost knowledge of his philosophy, revealed himself capable of nothing but theories—a critic and not a creator of life.

Whether this encounter in unconsciousness was the result of a wholly personal hallucination, or whether both had been, in their sleep, summoned towards each other by the power of desire, and whether, while she visited him, he, in turn, had gone to her—all this he could not unravel.

Yet he knew the import and the frequency of these mutual evocations and his soul was a battlefield where mysticism had instantly vanquished incredulity.

He went to stroll along the quais. The winter sun smiled, the wind had abated, sparrows chirped on the leafless trees, a warm humidity vaporized the mild air.

Books, first, passed before his eyes as far off and inaccessible things; then a binding tempted his hand, an unknown title, his attention. He felt the first titillations of fever, and gave himself up.

Now, one by one, he touched them, opened them, to acquire the certainty of the nothingness within; he grieved that a pleasant golden binding enclosed the gallant nonsense of little shivering verses of indigence, or the philosophism of a Diderot, or the worthless manuals of Jansenistic piety.

For a few sous he had just bought a treatise on simony and haggled eagerly with a rogue of a vendor for some Neo-Parnassian collections—recently received and already depreciated by the universal indifference—when a familiar hand was placed on his shoulder.

With a twisting movement, with a natural but sure insolence, he freed himself, then turned his head.

It was Marguerin, the theosophist, whose friends excused his licentious folly as a malady of the cerebellum. His play of features, strangely promising, seduced women in search of debasement: he was rich and subsidized an angelical review. This day, a fixed idea, which he confided to Entragues, gave his face an imbecile appearance.

"Dead! Perhaps you remember that blond girl, Maia!"

"His present phantasy," thought Hubert, "does not incite any repugnance. Have I not had the madness of eyes, and am I cured of it? Has not the vision of two large eyes ever been necessary to complete my happiness? It is strange that there should be this constant union of two sensations so different in kind, namely, visual sensation and spasm. Sick, ah! an innate and uncurable sickness!"

(*While sipping absinthe.*)

"Intoxication is a very noble passion, and I would like to acquire it.... Intoxication, one should rather say drunkenness, but philanthropists, have brought the word down to the humanitarian mud of their Anglican dissertations.... Alcoholism has been contaminated, no less.... Intoxication suffices. This absinthe is comforting. The blond Maia was perhaps loved by that wretch. She was lovely and here is what is left of it: a pathological regret. Why disdain intoxication? It is the most intellectual of passions; it does not depress like gambling; it does not weaken like love. Ah! what a godsend! Absinthe is not at all hurtful; it is green and concentrated wine. Is it not ideal to be able to arrive at intoxication with a single glass of liquid? The Orientals have opium, but for that is needed the Oriental sky. And then, to each one his own system. The important thing is that it remove you far from the world: everything that draws us away from ourselves is divine. How many times nevertheless, have I been drunk with pure contemplation! yes, that too is a method. All are salutary. I hate myself, I wish to live another life, I wish to correct ideally the infirmities inherent in my carnal state, I wish to deliver my soul from the miseries of my body ... I should love her from afar, as Guido loves his madonna. Contact is a destroyer of dreams. You will not know the book of love where I have beatified you, for it will disappear with desire, burned by the flames of your first kiss. The pyre that will open heaven for you will consume my forces: you will ascend upward through space and I will fall like Satan, I will fall into the infernal hells for eternity.... A singular declamation and quite difficult to justify! All this for some pleasure mutually shared by two beings who adore each other. The consequences of the union of the sexes are not at all so tragic, ordinarily ... I am very much upset. It is quite urgent that the denouement restores security to one of the actors. To bring things back to their true state: she will be troubled and I will be calmed—a very desirable result.

"For the aim of an intelligent life is not to live with the Princess of Trebizond, but to explain oneself in one's motives of action by deeds or by gestures. Writing reveals the inward act; it is much less important to feel than to know the order of sensation, and this is the mind's revenge on the body: nothing exists save through the Word. As well say that the Word alone exists. Saint John, the evangelist, knew it, and the Rajah Ramohun Roy knew it, and others: Om and Logos: it is the only science; when that is known everything is known. I will realize myself, accordingly, through the Word.... And you? What shall I do with you and your soul! Ah! Sixtine, your soul I shall drink, little by little, in nightly and daily celebrations, diluted in the saliva of your kisses,—like holy portions: you will have no existence save in me, and you will fortify me like a spiritual elixir. We shall be hermaphrodites. Thus will unity be brought about: and I shall have renounced, without renouncing you, the chimerical pursuit of a love external to myself. Ah! unity will not be ternary—sin against the rites! For I do not want carnal posterity. May my flesh be sterile and my mind fruitful! We shall beget dreams and with our thoughts we shall people the night of space. We shall talk, and our speech, diffused beyond the stars, will make the gloomy eternity of the ether vibrate eternally. We shall have gestures of love, and the signs of our love will be reflected in the innumerable mirrors of the molecules of light. Yes, we shall amuse ourselves with this illusion, in overturning Laws, by our phantasy, for we are not ignorant of the fact that the world dies of the caducity of thought which creates it and that the stars, as well as the nail of our little finger, will perish when death closes the eyes of the last man.

"Ah! I mount very high, I go very far. Like a bomb my head is filled with explosives and the lucidity of my mind grows extremely bright.... Then the novel will be vanquished: a new form of analysis will have been demonstrated. The identity of character will be affirmed by its very contradictions and something Hegelian will relieve the gloomy simplicity of ordinary creatures clothed in the rigidity of a material style. The novel of hearts, the novel of souls, the novel of bodies, the novel of all the sensibilities: after this must come the novel of minds. As I understand it, the word 'soul' represents the quintessence of heart; mind, that is to say pure intelligence in conflict with carnal inconveniences, was disdained, without doubt, as uninteresting. Always, and nothing but this, conjunctions of sexes and joy. Oh! well! quite natural! 'to possess the woman one loves.' But at last there are modern Antonies who have proposed other pur-poses to themselves, who have reduced all duties to a single duty—to conform one's life to one's dream. Passersby who jostle you proceed dreaming of the universal idealism as seriously as you of the surprises of perfected corsets. And some of them, if the beast asks for oats will answer: 'Death's white horse did not eat any of it.' And do you not suppose that if humiliating forces curve their refractory knees before a woman, they will not have, very often, recourse to the consolation of inward irony? In fine, I affirm the cerebral life—and all the rest was written in manuals of psychology.

"Irony is but a momentary protest, a mental destruction and a pledge against the excess of sensual satisfaction; it is not a certain way of liberation. From this halting-place one gradually mounts to a dominating position by pride or by contemplation, by art or by mysticism. These methods, known in their principle, are denied, like fairy-like childishness: in the novel they must be given the importance they have in daily life: As an animal, man thought only of perfecting his animalism; and Christianity was, one thinks, a notable spiritual advance. It endowed simple humanity with a complex soul. When Flaubert wrote *Salammbô*, he instinctively made the young priestess a Carmelite rather than a Vestal, for the Vestal obeys an order and the Carmelite a love; one is attached to her position through habit, the other through love. The idyl, the satire of customs, the picaresque romance, the tragic and fatal passion, the patriotic epic, the amorous plaint,—the ancients had no other literature: the first histories of a soul, the first analytical novel was spontaneously born in the new genius of a Christianized mind and it was Saint Augustine who wrote it. Modern literature commences with the *Confessions*.

"We must return to it. Zola and others may continue to catalogue their inferior animals, they have no interest for us: they are crude creatures about to acquire light, chrysalid intelligences: we are little concerned with the quality of the food with which they gorge themselves, or with their pruriencies. Whatever is not intellectual is foreign to us.

"What a disconcerting irony that in this century which drinks the blue democratic wine from the Chalice, no original prose writer was revealed who was not Christian by instinct or belief, desire or necessity, love or disgust,— from Chateaubriand to Villiers and Huysmans, and no true poet, from Vigny to Baudelaire and Verlaine!

"Comte has not touched, with his heavy stones, the souls he wanted to overwhelm,—no more than an infant who hurls tiny pebbles from the strand at the inaccessible flight of gulls! And this very age, which claims to admit only the force that is mathematically proved, will be extinguished by verbal idealism. People will no longer believe in things, but in the mere ideas we have of them; and, as the obscurity of the idea is clarified only by speech, nothing more of things will exist than the words describing them and the final destruction of matter will end with the judgment of this axiom: The universe is the sign of the word...."

"But," reflected Hubert again, as he left the *café*, "this, and my scorn of a derisive reality and illusive truth, does not imply laziness in art, or cowardice, or the approximate. Nor has the idealism I profess anything in common with the vague intuitions of those spinners of psychological ribbons,—it is a documented idealism, solidly erected, like the ornamented portal of a cathedral, upon the foundations of accuracy...."

CHAPTER XXXIII

AN EVENING IN SOCIETY

"En résumé, la fête me paraissait un bal
de fantômes."
Villiers de l'Isle-Adam,
l'Amour suprême.

Hubert gladly mingled in the conversations, dances, scandals, the many (rather charming) frivolities which took place from eleven o'clock in the evening until six o'clock in the morning at the home of the Countess Aubry.

Flowers, music, vocal screeches and caresses, shoulders, diamonds, bedizened uniforms, for the countess had connections with foreign diplomacy.

Sixtine, an augural apparition, appeared through the clinking Japanese portiere; one of her hands played with her multicolored pearls.

She advanced, Moscowitch behind her, his eyes fixed on her pure shoulders. His huge stature dominated the young woman by a whole head; he walked after her and Sixtine, faltering, seemed a very little girl kept in leading-strings by a giant. Hubert, with a bow of impertinent familiarity, passed between them and offered Sixtine his arm towards a chair. The Russian, resigned, joined a group of men and watched the talkers.

"You looked as though you were under the guardianship of that strong man, and I wanted to deliver you."

She began to laugh, quite an enigmatical laugh:

"No, he doubtless followed me for pleasure, wanting to have me under his eyes. Can a woman at a ball do anything better than let herself be seen?"

"And is it not a keen pleasure," returned Hubert, "to reveal one's arms, shoulders and neck?..."

"Very keen, no, but really the desires one evokes murmur in the ears like a flight of vernal butterflies and the rustling of their wings is sometimes soothing to the skin. You cannot understand, it is too feminine."

"Yes," murmured Hubert with a tender but undeniable irony. "Woman is a religion full of mysteries. I wish merely to adore without understanding, to kneel in the gloom, my eyes unraised towards the symbolic little red lamp: joyous mysteries and sad mysteries, to contemplate them alternatively, to know them never, perhaps, in their secret essence, and to love the dear creature whose emanation they are."

She raised her saddened eyes towards him, then, with a little anger:

"Poet and lying poetry! Tenderness is on your lips and not in your heart. Do you remember our first meeting, under the drooping branches of the old sacred firs, down there, in the gloomy avenue? You declared that nothing exists except through an evoking will. I remember it, and since then your words, often meditated, have acquired a terrible and clear meaning. You love a dream creature which you have incarnated under a semblance which is mine; you do not love me as I am, but as you have made me. You do not love a woman, but a heroine of a romance, and everything for you is but a romance.... I will tell you about this at greater length some other time, if I have leisure. Ah! my friend, there often is much charm in you, ah! if you wished and if you knew!... Do something to make me love you sufficiently to resign myself to be loved as the moving shadow of a dream. Do this ... but what do I know? To-morrow, I shall perhaps give you merely a brief no. Perhaps it will be too late to-morrow. Trust no woman, even the sincerest. Their flight is as capricious as the flight of a swallow; this one flies, that one.... They go whither their caprice takes them and then ... and then they follow the sun and kisses are fascinating beams.... Do you find that I seem to be giving you a course in seduction, according to my practice. Ah! perhaps it would be better were you contented with the dream. You could shape it according to your desire, while I, for example, will I not be malleable in vain, if I revolt against your candor? Good-by, the countess has beckoned to me and you know that I am her right hand on all grand occasions.... Good-by, Hubert, oh! we shall doubtless meet once or twice in the course of the evening.... Why not? We have so many things to say to each other.... Give me your arm."

"Strange creature, yet you belong to me! Inextricable problem, I shall decipher you by force of love, for love is the golden key which opens all women's hearts. You have the evangelical good will, you wish to love, you will love, and whom could you love except me? I shall have the curiosity to admit all your phantasies, even those which make me suffer; I do not dislike torture: this helps one to reflect on the inconveniences of being a man."

"Are you enjoying yourself?"

It was Calixte, satisfied to exhale his ennui with this simple interrogation.

"I am not bored, first, for secret reasons, then, there are some pretty dresses. It would be pleasant perhaps to imagine the nude; it is quite another matter to contemplate it: not one woman in ten gives the slightest desire to see more of her. One can be diverted for an hour or two in phonographing some fragments of the conversations in one's memory. But it is too early; this becomes somewhat eccentric only around two o'clock in the morning.

"And also," said Calixte, "to trouble some naive hearts with burning avowals."

"Ah!" answered Hubert, "are you become a dilettante? Yes, this is quite a sadistic pleasure...."

"Nevertheless...."

"Oh!" continued Hubert, "the casuists, whom fools scorn, were profound analysts of human nature. They gave concessions to love which the modern Malthusians find extreme, the hypocrites! And in this is manifest their wisdom and a marvellous intuition about physiological needs. There is not a kiss which the disdainful boldness of Ligouri does not concede to the sadness of flesh; nothing astonishes him and he condemns the most complex satiations as only venial, provided the dignity of the act be consecrated by the supreme finality."

Calixte was too spontaneous to like casuistry.

"Destiny," he told Hubert, "should have made you a monk in a Spanish monastery of the sixteenth century."

"Ah!" acquiesced Hubert, "with the grace of God I should have written fine folios."

"But you are living in the world, in an age little given to procreation, and if you put your theories to practice...."

"You well know," interrupted Hubert, "that I am, practically, abstemious, and one need not take account of accidents. Ho! I should not dislike to have some progeniture. If life were better, it would be justifiable; if it were good, it would be a strict commandment. But I have the consciousness of my wretchedness and this will spare existence to the generations who might have issued from me. Do you know my principle? It is short, strict, and I would wish it universal: No children."

Renaudeau and André de Passavant approached.

"Oh!" continued Hubert, "practically, it would be absurd and terrible, but, the principle admitted, its too numerous violations would suffice for an always excessive peopling. I should accept this cross, if it were necessary. My children would bear life as I bear it, without joy but without despair. The transcendent rascal has not killed all the swans!"

"Not yet, but he will kill them all," said André. "The lakes will be deserted and the forests silent, for they no longer will have souls to people the lakes with dreams and the forests with ideal music. Then fire will lay waste the terrestrial marsh...."

"And we shall begin again at the beginning," interrupted Renaudeau.

He disappeared without adding anything further, and Passavant, who followed him with his eyes, explained this sudden flight by seeing him glide swiftly towards Madame Aubry, who was smiling at him:

"They claim that he has already succeeded in undermining Fortier and that he is going to replace him in the review, if it is not already effected—and elsewhere, naturally."

"It was to be foreseen," said Hubert. "But as for myself, I shall not submit to his impertinences. If a few friends wished to follow me, I should sacrifice whatever sums were necessary to start a magazine that will be stricter in its choosing."

"And slightly theological?" added Passavant.

"Mystic theology in fine style...."

"Yes, yes," responded Hubert, suddenly absent-minded.

He instantly recalled that the present imposed other thoughts upon him. For the first time in his life, perhaps, he escaped the exclusive domination of art. Sixtine arose before his vision of the world like a gigantic tree whose boughs and shadows conceal the thick woods stretching behind it.

"What! Baillot here!" said Passavant, shocked.

"What has he done to you?" asked Calixte.

"Do you not remember that he denounced Desnoyers, the architect of Mont Saint-Michel, as a clerical?"

"I have seen," said Hubert, "his restorations, and they are admirable. When the years will have covered the too fresh richness with its patina, they will be masterpieces marvelously harmonizing with the architectural creations of ancient time. But I believe that it is just because he is a believer that he was able to reconstitute, as much by love as by science, such superb testimonies of a Christian epoch. What would you, a Maecenas was needed and they got a pedant!"

At this moment, Moscowitch found himself face to face with Entragues. The Russian knitted his eyebrows, but a smile, at the same instant, extenuated it:

"My dear, for the moment I renounce my dramatic projects. This damp winter is unfavorable to me, and I am going to pass a few months in the south. Thanks for all your excellent advice. They have helped me beyond your hopes."

This tone of haughty irony displeased Entragues, who answered:

"Take care, Monsieur. Are you so sure of being at such a stage where absence cannot injure you? Do you leave with the certainty of receiving letters of recall? Think that more than another I am interested in a denouement to which I have not been a stranger. Calixte, my friend, give Monsieur Moscowitch a commentary of the thirty-fourth chapter of Stendhal. Madame Magne, I think, has a word to tell me, and I am going to her."

He had perceived Sixtine visibly bored by some fool's compliments.

"At least," he thought, "she will be thankful to me for having delivered her."

Moscowitch patiently listened to Calixte whose amusing discourse on discretion yet seemed to him a contrived raillery. During this torture, Hubert sought to resume his interrupted talk with Sixtine. But she was distracted and almost meditative. Hubert related to her the poetry of his desire and she gazed at him, without having the air of understanding. Playing with her dance card, she said:

"You have not even had the idea of putting your name here and I am no longer free. Those who have requested to dance with me will come, each in proper turn, to claim the promised minutes, and, you see, it is full."

Hubert took the little card and read the inscribed names:

"Well, sacrifice one of these persons for me, the Russian for example. That would be specially agreeable."

"No," said Sixtine, "that is not possible."

"I see that you take to the man, even more than to his portrait."

"What portrait?"

"That one signed with initials which belongs to your name, and which was dedicated, still in abbreviation, to Monsieur Sabas Moscowitch...."

"Ah! that amusement of a rainy afternoon?... Is my past not sacred to you, then?"

"It dismays me. What I do not know bewilders me ... I want to know."

"But what do you gain by tormenting me thus? And by what right do you ask such questions? You are wicked to make me suffer in my soul and flesh. Leave me, or I shall tell you cruel things ..."

"I can listen to them."

"No, really, I am tired, ah! how tired I am!"

And her eyes repeated the avowal of her lips.

"But," she continued, "let us have a truce, I want to amuse myself, I want to forget, in purely nervous excitements, the struggle I am engaged with. Leave me to my partners and come to-morrow. I am very much disturbed. Come with confidence: no one has as many privileges with me as you have, Hubert, but think of all that can happen in a second, a single brief second. Here is Monsieur de Fortier come to claim me.... *A demain!*"

Then, instead of rejoining his friends, he strolled about, insinuating himself into groups, watching, listening.

A young girl, thin and ugly, despite large dark eyes, was languidly dreaming in a chair. The fancy seized him to amuse this child. He bowed to her and the young girl, heedless of etiquette, let herself be lifted into these strange arms. The waltz made her little heart beat, her pale cheeks grew rosy, she pressed Entragues hand and in the boldness of pleasure let her bent and radiant head fall on his shoulder. He made her chat, treated her as a woman, conducted her to the refreshment-room, made her tipsy with a little champagne and a few compliments: he was thanked with a smile, which expressed the gift of a life.

In bringing her back to her place, he was almost as happy as she was and he thought that the only happiness lies in giving happiness without demanding a return.

Towards two o'clock, he resisted Calixte Heliot who discreetly tried to draw him away. Later, he saw Moscowitch, after consulting his watch, disappear into the antechamber. Sixtine brushed past him at the same instant; she turned around, chattering, on the arm of Renaudeau, who seemed to be telling her something malicious. For an hour, perhaps more, he remained in the same place, alone and motionless, watching her pass from hand to hand, carefree and smiling. He watched with an empty brain, rendered anaemic by the late hour, fuddled by the incessant bustle. Finally the rooms began to thin. While he was hesitating to offer himself to Sixtine as an escort, she vanished, flying, without turning her head, like a woman quite decided to refuse or to accept only with boredom and bad grace the arm of a man.

He suffered her to leave, went to compliment the countess, bowed to the young girl who gave him her hand, drank a last glass of punch, so as to be less affected by the morning chill, then departed in his turn and returned on foot to his dwelling.

CHAPTER XXXIV

POETIC RAPTURE

"Quand le monde fait peur, quand la foule fatigue.
Quand le coeur n' a qu'un cri:—Te voir, te voir, te voir!"
Mme. Desbordes-Valmore.

He rose late, enjoying, through the window whose curtains were lifted, the wintry charm of a pale noon sun, and delighting in the state of half-consciousness which follows, after an irregular night, an extremely physical fatigue. His anaemia of a transplanted plant, combatted and almost vanquished by a regime that was country-like, returned on such mornings. He felt the languor of the consumptive and the melancholia of the adolescent.

The substantial breakfast arranged by his maid was less a comfort to his fatigued organs than an intoxication. The smoking of a single cigarette turned his head: he acquired, without having sought it, an exquisite beatitude. It was like a new condition of animated matter: the dissolving state—a special enjoyment reserved for lazy sleepers and late breakfasters. Brief, like all delights, it was not long in waning, but it was transformed gradually into an agreeable sensation of peace.

Then, stretching an arm towards his Gothic Bible, he removed the copper clasp and read, in a cloud of blue smoke, drinking strong coffee in little sips, the aphorisms of Ecclesiastes.

A reading decidedly proper to lift a wise man far above other men, a cup where one drinks sheer emptiness as surely as in a cupule of lotus, ah! ideal banalities, written, without a doubt, for the days that follow festivals.

FORTITUDE

"Poverty, labor, bodily miseries, bleeding heart wounds, bitterness of bread and wine,

"Repose, suppleness, flowerings, embraces, warmth of joyous repasts,

"And all, and all vibrations.

"The cerebral enlightenment:

"All this indifferent to us, from the commencement to the end,

"For there is a commencement and an end, and, thank God, the soothing void is made for all.

"We have confidence in the transcendental goodness of the Creator: he will not prolong, beyond the human term, our pains or joys.

"And not even a shrugging of shoulders, for we are too witty to rage against the eternal laws; besides, we have the sentiment of decorum."

He was tired, as tired as Sixtine, of this dim passion. The night of their hearts truly needed some flashes of lightning. For a week she had retired within herself, but like a flower which, at the approach of a storm, draws together its trembling petals above the sacred pistils; the danger over, they return to their former state and joyously receive the fugitive caress of the passing pollen.

"Another less metaphorical reflection: the Russian has certainly made positive advances and in his plaints the magic word of marriage must, like an echo, have returned and reverberated. Magic he considers it. I do not know. She must wish to preserve a certain liberty of behavior and the personal home of a woman unaccustomed to share the ambient air with another. Moreover, I have never surprised, in the implications of her phrases, the least allusion to a matrimonial desire. I do not believe that she would wish to close with such a banal epilogue the indefinite avenue of our common dreams. We cannot erect this barrier in the midst of our life, dividing in two adverbs—before, after—the perspective of our desires, that sphinx rising towards the horizontal profundities of the sky!

"Ah! I regret that this is not the stone on which her foot has stumbled, for I should understand at least.

"After all, she was only to answer me. I think that I have been sufficiently precise and if acts rather than words were needed, have I not given myself up to acts?

"A quite unfortunate tentative!...

"Ah! I am weary, as weary as she is weary.

"If you do not wish to drink the dew I offer to your lips in the hollow of my hand, some beast, bolder or wiser, will pass, that will refresh itself with this drink of love.

"Come while it is morning and while animal life sleeps in the woods!

"Come to roam among the wet herbs: I will shake off the rain of pearls and the snow flakes of diamonds from your blond hair!

"Come and you will exult with joy, come, the train of your robe, among the mosses, will make a wake of light, and the rising sun will kiss, in its candor, the smile of your purple lips!

"Come, you will be as a white-browed queen among green branches, and the tame butterflies will rest on your ears.

"You will subdue nature and at the call of your mouth, my soul, wild as a fawn, will bound towards you."

Analyses and dithyrambs formulated the same slavery. He wished to make this woman happy, to see her eyes drawn back and her lips, by the oppression of an emotion, opened. The evocation was suddenly effected, not, it is true, under the direct visual form, but in a far away vaporous and voluptuous world. Kneeling near her, after the last evolutions of the embrace, he contemplated her.

"Truly my life is transferred into this woman as under the attraction of a magnet, and truly the center of my forces is in that heart!

"Those blond lashes of her blue eyes are the chains of my days, and the blond shadow of her hair is the halo of bright moons whose splendor illumines my nights."

He would have proceeded at greater length, for his words were unleased, but the vision vanished.

"Presage: Ah! pretty beast! ah! pretty beast!"

Then he reflected again:

"All this has been badly managed. I should have designed, as Calixte suggested, this woman in the pure rôle of a Beatrice exempt from carnal affairs,—but being a woman, she would not have understood: Beatrice, who lent herself to this sublime play, was a dream creature, obeying the poet and the very symbol of his thought. This one had to fall into my arms, or other arms would have snatched her.

"Remain on your pedestal. It is on my knees that I wish to adore you, my hands outstretched to you, eternally.

"No, I grow weary, up there. Adorer, adore nearer, adore with kisses.

"Well! at least we shall have some moments of pleasant intimacy and since it is necessary to make an object of pleasure out of the object of worship, let the sacrilege be complete and the voluptuousness decisive.

"Ah! I shall abandon myself to your body of illusions. Excellent and noble substance, you will be kneaded according to the most transcendental phantasies!"

CHAPTER XXXV

THE ADORER

V.—The Visitation

"Vous qui parlez d'un ton si doux
En m'annoncant de bonnes choses,
Ma Dame, qui donc êtes-vous?
Verlaine, *Sagesse*.

"Yes, beloved Guido, I am the Queen of Angels, the Archangelic Virgin, the Morning Star, the Tower of David, the Golden House, I am...."

"Oh! no, you are the Novella, do not frighten me, I need all my presence of mind."

"Well, whatever you wish, but I love you. Close your eyes, I am inviolate and I feel myself blush. What will you think of me? Alas! it is really true that no one has ever implored me in vain. I cannot resist love's invocations, and when I am called with faith, I open the portal of heaven, and an angel lifts me on his wings."

"Adored Madonna," murmured Guido, kissing feet that were pure as the dew, "I am unworthy of your favors and see, my kisses are full of tears. Virgin of all love, my love was but a drop of water, and you have taken it in the holy lily of your heart. Be blessed for your goodness."

The Novella stooped towards the prisoner and touched his face with her lips.

She removed her crown of stars: the stars took wings to the roof and made a firmament of it. The buckle of her girdle hung in the air like a sun and the clasp of her cloak became a moon of white nights.

She sighed deeply, and from her lips was born a cloud that veiled the beaming glory of the stars with a vague charm. Then she said:

"Guido, you have doubted, look and die of love!"

She blossomed into a mystic rose that exhaled an adorable perfume.

And Guido's heart was filled with sweetness.

Then she became a pure mirror in which flamed a sword.

And Guido's heart was filled with justice.

Then she became a throne of cedar where graven sentences could be read.

And Guido's heart was filled with wisdom.

Then a vase appeared which was of bronze, then of silver, then of gold; from it issued clouds of incense of cinnamon and of myrrh.

And Guido's heart was filled with adorations.

Then uprose a tower of ivory and other visions, then a resplendent portal which Guido recognized as the portal of heaven, and he commenced to wonder whether this adventure would not finish as speciously as his adventure with Pavona.

Yet his heart was filled with joy.

"No, no, no. I belong to the angels. Die, become an angel, throw off this flesh which would soil me, assume the celestial form, and we shall see, Guido. Remember that I am inviolate. I repeat, I belong to the angels.... You have seen this!"

And with this last irony, the Most Prudent Virgin disappeared, as she had come, through the lock.

An aromatic odor filled the cell. Guido delightedly inhaled these virginal remains, then told himself:

"She is right, I must die. Besides, I owe her a visit."

CHAPTER XXXVI

ANGER

"Lui ne vous connait plus. Vous l' Ombre déjà vue
Vous qu' il avait couchée en son ciel tout nue,
Quand il était un Dieu...."
Tristan Corbière, *les Amours jaunes*.

It was the maid who made inquiries. She knew nothing, did not understand. Madame had certainly returned, but the bed had not been used, only rumpled, as if she had lain upon it fully dressed. The closet was open and the dressing table in an unwonted disorder, for Madame had never failed to place all her little belongings carefully.

"I should say," she continued, "that Madame has left for a trip on the go, as you might say, but I have not found the ball dress. No one goes far in a ball dress! When I came down at seven o'clock, things were as I have told you and since then I have been waiting, very uneasy, I assure you. And does Monsieur know nothing?"

"Nothing," answered Entragues. "She must have returned about half past four, or at five o'clock at the most. But come, if she had left for a trip, at least a street dress would be missing, a hat, some necessary objects, and especially a traveling bag, a valise."

"The bags, valises and trunks are above a dark closet, near my room. She would have to pass through my room to get to it. As for dresses and the rest, the wardrobe is locked with a key and I do not know where the keys are. But Madame always carries them with her."

Entragues asked:

"Are you sure that she returned?"

"She did return. After Madame's departure, yesterday, I put everything in order, I even smoothed the bed in which she had thrown herself for a moment after dinner. It is Madame's habit when she goes to a ball. And this morning the bed was disordered. Yet Madame is not heavy, and usually, when she sleeps, one can hardly see the mark of her body."

"Well," said Entragues, giving his address and a few coins to the maid, "if you learn anything, come and tell me. I am as uneasy as you are, Azélia. Come to-morrow morning, at any rate, perhaps I shall have news."

He departed. In the street, his calm grew agitated.

"I am deceived," he cried, "scandalously deceived!"

He opened his umbrella so violently that the silk snapped; then he smashed it against the edge of the sidewalk, threw it into the gutter, and, under the heavy and frigid fog, reached the end of the boulevard Saint-Germain, near the quai Saint-Bernard.

There, in a blind alley, amid huts, stood a little furnished house, patronized by Russian students and having the name of the Hôtel de Moscow.

"Monsieur Moscowitch."

"Monsieur Moscowitch left this morning for Nice. Does Monsieur wish his address? Grand Hôtel des Deux-Mondes."

"Thank you."

"The hotel is good, well situated. I spent a pleasant week there, the other winter. If I had known of your decision, Madame, I should have recommended the room I occupied, for the view through its sunny windows is delightful. Ah! just a year ago from to-day. I am becoming tranquil!"

He slowly walked as far as the boulevard Saint-Michel, under the pitiless rain which now fell in fine and penetrating needles.

"This Russian was imprudent in giving his address in advance! For I might go to trouble the first peace of this improvised honey-moon by a duel. So, at midnight she gives me a rendezvous for the next evening at her home, and at five o'clock in the morning she yields to Moscowitch in her own home, in her ball dress, and at about seven o'clock the two lovers take the express for Nice. Either it was well planned, and she decoyed me shamefully or, as I think, it is a matter of an impromptu affair and she held her modesty of soul in contempt so as to repel me. It is evident that Moscowitch waited for her at the door of the Aubry mansion, in a carriage, and that she let herself be carried off. Ah! he is a clever rascal. I am quite anxious to have some details. If he really followed my ironic advice, if the plan I gave him was good, I am ... I am truly below the most naive school boy. Well! there still remains for me the satisfaction of a dilettante: I have not myself won the battle, but like a staff-chief major general, I have directed the victory's course. Yes, in short, I am the organizer of my own defeat.... Now, it is a matter of producing a strict reasoning and not to lose myself in the by-ways of analysis. A proof? There is none, or not yet. I should, to the very end, respect the dignity of my sentiment. Coincidences, probabilities, but in the end she will give me an explanation. Then I shall judge. What reproaches? She has followed her pleasure."

He entered a café where warm drinks comforted him. At this moment he perceived that he was pierced with cold and that his hands were shivering. It was not only with cold that, he trembled, but his pride would not admit it and haughtily clothed itself in the cloak of irony. He did not even admit that his heart could bleed under a real wound; the griefs where he condescended to quench his original thirst were divine, voluntary, and not the work of a human hand. He possessed to a high degree the art of crucifying and stigmatizing himself, like a visionary, of leading his wounded heart to frightful tortures, to a slow agony; he had the art of being his own executioner. He had voluntarily sweated with anguish, but that the gentle thrust of a woman's delicate gauntlet should drive the crown of thorns into his skull, no, no, no! "For after all, complicity is essential to suffering and it must be voluntary; and that is a favor no creature will ever obtain from me."

Quite honestly, he reflected:

"At least it was brief and the commencement, middle and end took three months. There are many days to revive in this trilogy of zodiacs. Thus, that first meeting which she, the traitress, recalled herself, yesterday evening. Residual sensations still vibrate in my nerves and I hear "the wind pass, stirring the dry leaves." May they sound in your ears, too, Sixtine, and may the sound of their pursuit sadden, like the tattoo of a rattle-snake, the "delicate landscape" where moves your captive soul! You asked to be plundered, treasure: well! now you are a prisoner of the flesh, adore your prison, your chains, and your jailer.

"This journey was for me the occasion of a return to my youth: these renewals are anthologies, but what if it were necessary to re-read the entire book, letter by letter! Oh! no, oh! no. And no more than the vendor of *almanachs de Leopardi*, will I give my consent: 'Oh! no! but another, monsieur, one quite new!' Ah! oxydized hearts aspiring after the virginity of a new stamp, you will fall into the crucible! Ah! patience, we shall enjoy the devouring liquefaction: and our molecules will return into the matrix and other coins of divinity will continue our broken circulation,—other coins eternally the same!

"Wretched logic: these three months of my life are dominated by an absurdity which will decide its disposition, like a lunar play in an old, used mirror.

"Sixtine, it will be good of you to tell me that legend, now that you no longer need reserve the charm of mysteries, this one and the other, you know which one, that of the poison!—Ah! to think that I shall never know it,—no more than the color of your eyes when they open to the morning light.

"When I returned to 'my enlarged room,' it was finished, you possessed me. But know that it was not without inward struggles and that many affections, already old, divided a large and profound heart. Also learn that at that time Madame du Boys was not without attractions for me, in her so ingenuously perverse naivete,—and had you not come, I should have made perhaps another little trip with her to Switzerland. Ah! but you have aped her! Sixtine, has your dignity consented to a surreptitious abduction? Send me a bouquet of violets by post!... I should have taught you the play of transcendental pleasantries, and you would have liked it. You are too serious, you really effect too much! You mistake accident for destiny; it is only a fragment. Shake off, then, the dust of eternity which illusion has sprinkled on your wings! Have you taken at least a return ticket? It is economical and gives a value to the landscape, for, without this precaution, one would never think of looking at it. 'We have plenty of time!'"

"If we had left together, we should first of all not have left at all, for what is the good of moving, since in every place one remains the same to himself. Then, as I know what to do about carnal values I should have spared you many irritating surprises. Finally ... ah! well, but is it not within my right to believe that I alone could have played the rôle?

"Before I found you, in your gestures, in the tacit consent of your good will—a consent quite momentary, it appears—my love had already found a parallel, incarnate in Guido della Preda. At this hour, his fate disquiets me seriously. Sixtine, you have a murder on your conscience (that will make two), for if I do not die it will be because Guido's death has spared my life.... Yes, he must die in my place....

"I saw you once again. The evening clothed itself in a charming minute, unique diamond whose resplendence has not left my night. It was when ... no, that is bitter. Ah! in the opening of that stone was an orient of psychic phantasmagories. It was full of softness and mildness and languor. Such moments have no morrow; also, it were better never to have lived in them. One pursues their sisters who stroll on the dial-plate, and this can lead far, to the very depths of the hells where gloomy victims lament over the *nessum maggior dolore*.

"In subsequent conversations, you appeared to me as a proud, intelligent and sensual amazon. Sensuality is the ferment of feminine nature: without this decisive gift, there might be angels, there would be no women. But it is quite true that I have not known how to awaken its might and my magnetism struck sudden neutralities. You are not a woman of good-will: your very pride leads you to inopportune resistance where force alone could be right! It is there that one is the dupe of one's intelligence! One must have the strength to throw it off, at certain hours, like a cloak or like the chemise of the Roman woman. For it was not the modesty which visits only extreme youth or the first ignorance: no, it was rather the intelligence. You wished to understand

and feel at the same time, and for this you took pains to keep your presence of mind. See how this coincided: I, on my side, made the same effort, with less pain perhaps. Both of us knew well what we wished, and our wills, lacking a little salutary unconsciousness were destroyed in their immobile efficacy.

"Nothing more. This is sufficient enlightenment."

(This was an infraction against his habits,—but a need of personal security forced him to hurl half of himself through the window, so as to preserve the integrity of the rest: in four hours of the night he reached the final point of what he now called "a foolish anecdote.")

CHAPTER XXXVII

THE ADORER

VI.—Memorare

"Memorare, pia Virgo, non esse auditum
a saeculo quemquam ad tau currentem
praesidia, tua implorantem auxilia, tua
petentem suffragia, a te esse derelictum."
Saint Bernard.

"My lord, my lord, hush! listen!" exclaimed Veltro during the ascent of the tower's staircase. "But do not betray me! I believe they are interceding for you, for the affair was infamous, if I know aught about it. To-morrow, my lord, to-morrow, you understand, I know that the order will come to open the door for you, but hush!"

"What?" Guido, atremble, questioned, "I shall be free to-morrow?"

"Yes, my lord, but that is enough on this subject. Only, I believe that your lordship owes a present to our holy madonna. She has rewarded your devotion, she has interceded; it is she, I am sure it is she...."

"Thank you, Veltro, you are a good man. The first ducats that are returned to me will be for the Novella, the second for you."

He hastened to the accustomed vision, but his limbs gave way, his hands glanced over the rope-support, his heart beat like the eternal clock; he required the effort of supreme will-power to overcome dizziness, to pass the last steps, to fall on his knees near the balustrade.

There, full of anguish, made giddy by the sudden rolling that shook the tower, like a ship amid storm, he felt himself fainting, then his eyes dimmed and he wept.

Indifferent as a madonna, the Novella watched him weep.

Then, without transition, he felt in his soul the rage that dismissed lovers feel.

"What have I done to you? Do you find that I did not love you with a sufficiently insatiable love? Come, you know well that I belong to you: do you recall the pact? Do you wish me to call you perjurer? Are you a woman, after all? Woman, but madonna, and I have no insults metaphysical enough to injure you. Yet, do not abuse your virginity, you will force yourself to say disagreeable things. Well, we are going to come to terms: take me as an orphan. Afterwards, we shall see."

Indifferent as a madonna, the Novella still watched him.

"Ah!" Guido thought, "she is inflexible. Her heart is an eternal decree. I rail at her who was before Time, how stupid! And I sink into blasphemous sarcasms which her son one day will charge me with. Passion leads me into error, but passion above all else!"

"Novella! adored madonna, listen to me. There have been times when you were more clement. I implore you, speak to me, give me a smile. No? Nothing? Ah! I am deserted! Think—I have but you. The white town straggling under your divine feet, the blue sea, your immortally dying sister, the firmament less pure than your inviolate soul, the roses which are the perfume of your most chaste thought, all that is charming in nature, I love as your emanation, as a perpetual Month of Mary. Ah! I shall recite to you the rosary of my griefs, and in the end I shall crucify myself to please you! You should at least be grateful for my reserve: was I not proper when you came to see me? Yet, you loved me that day, and what if I had really insisted, O permanent Virgin?...

"How beautiful you are! Ah! wonder-working beauty, sacred beauty! Ah! it is not in vain that the Infinite has dwelt in your bosom: your smile is impregnated with it forever. But you no longer wish to smile....

"Comfort me, through pity, since it is written in your anthems. Are you now going to encourage scepticism? If you truly are the consoler of afflicted souls, prove it, for I am full of affliction. Yes, I feel that it is a wretched reasoning: you do what you wish and your auxilliary grace has devolved only on those of good will. I reason too much. It is not thus that one touches the heart of a woman, O woman of women, am I not right?

"Yet I would like, before dying, once again to recall this to you: 'Recollect that you have never been implored in vain!' If you have no condescension for my love, have some for my madness. Do you not perceive that I ramble incoherently, and to what point. What would you, it is thus when one loves!

"So, we are going to separate....

"Ah! virginal purples! star-like dawns! Ah! early mornings and late tendernesses! Illusive universe, begone, shameful Satan repulsing my caresses! She has smiled! Again, again! She opens her arms to me! Ah! God! is it possible? Yes, I knew it. Ah! of words, nothing is closed to verbal incantations. On what does happiness depend?

"She opens her arms to me, she loves me. Here I am, here! How I am going to adore you, how I am going to recite lovely litanies to you, and all the essential orisons. Nothing separated me from you but your will, and your will accepts me, finally cleansed of human defilement by the baptism of blood. Joy more indefinable than the immaculate conception, the virgin of virgins opens to the sinner the ivory portals of pure love...."

Dreaming of such things, Guido leaped over the balustrade, precipitantly towards the madonna who awaited him, laughing and with outstretched arms.—*Ave, Rosa speciosa!*

CHAPTER XXXVIII

PRIDE

"... Voire mesme que si un de nos confraires
se monstroit attaché à quelque chose,
qu'il en soit aussistost privé...."
Règle de S. Benoist, ch. xxxviii.

When Azélia presented herself the next morning, her face bearing the marks of tears and trouble, for "she was now sure that Madame had been murdered; never had Madame gone away so long without notifying her," Entragues was able to reassure her:

"Madame is at Nice, in the Grand Hôtel des Deux-Mondes. She arrived there yesterday evening, is in splendid health and finds that the sea is blue, so blue! And the palms and the flowers! Everything is fragrant. Never before has she felt how sweet life is!"

"So Monsieur has received a telegram. Ah! good. But to leave without telling me! If Madame writes, I shall communicate with Monsieur, for Madame loves Monsieur very much."

"Yes, we are, as they say, a pair of friends."

A day passed, then another, and Hubert grew really bored. It was the sensation of emptiness usually felt by all sensitive creatures in like occurrences.

The light had fled from him; he moved in deserts of dark expanses.

No distraction is possible, since the only being from whom pleasure could come has withdrawn from the visual field, since the generating soul of all joy has fled, since the beams have perished, since the night of absence reigns.

He could have lived near her, removed by a distance of several streets, without any great need of visiting. The possibility of a meeting, the certainty of a welcome sufficed for the vitality of his desires. Here rises the tyranny of the Spirit of Contradiction and its immutable disdain for the present hour. Moralists have always quarreled with man on this matter: "You do not know how to enjoy the fugitive minute." No, but how go about it, since it would be necessary that the fugitive minute suspend its flight, it would be necessary that it exist. Now, it is a vulgar idea that only the past or the future has an appearance of objectivity: the moment never comes to pass.

Hubert had not even the liberty for such elementary deductions. He suffered like an exile, a pure suffering and with a fixed idea. Jealousy in no way troubled its undulations: it was the unique sensation of the lost object. His joy, fallen into the sea, was lying under moving waves; with each wave the diamond was engulfed in the sands more deeply, and he could not yet anticipate the tempest which would throw it on the surface, tossing it to the strand among the eternal pebbles.

Ah! the solitary dream house among the dunes had indeed fallen to his lot suddenly and too soon. He had not had time to arrange his parcels, to bring the least illusion—more bare of spiritual comfort than a hermit in the desert—of lust.

Such a state of soul brought about this reaction: "I am perhaps deceived in the value of these coincidences. Well, I must not despair."

He delighted in this self-contempt for several hours, inhaling his baseness and wallowing in it as in warm mire. Yet there were instants of respite, and in the evening he walked tranquilly, with a normal step, towards the dwelling of the absent one, but restless as a man who is expected.

Azélia opened the door before he rang.

"Monsieur! ah! just look!"

And she drew a letter from her dress.

"Madame has written me, and this is for you."

The white envelope with the oblique water-marks bore no writing.

"This is prudence!"

At the pressure of his fingers, he felt a very thin English onion-skin paper within.

"She has written me a volume here. Ah! Prolixity! Would a word not have sufficed?—Adieu!"

Hubert was very calm as he received this sentence of death, and his indifference, perfectly acted, although for himself, scandalized the good Azélia.

She believed in kisses, thought that he would press the object to his heart, ejaculating some words of tenderness, as in the romances and chromos, which are painted romances.

With a "thank you!" he placed the letter in his pocket and, pushing a door open, entered the little room in whose corners his dying illusions still played, like ironic dryads, careless of the approaching agony.

"*Moriuntur ridendo.*"

A light voiceless laugh came from him:

"These are the ruins of Carthage. They are well preserved and yet how many centuries is it since we left them, already in the state of ruins. Within me generations have succeeded; the same essence of humanity reigns, the man is another man. Ah! how far away all this is!

"These objects were once familiar to me: I knew them. I was a little their master. They have escaped my hands. Well! I abandon the rest. Let all things be transitory. How this breathes of death! It is my heart that is becoming decomposed....

"Why read the letter? She laughs at me or pities me, and never have I tolerated the one or the other."

He carried it through the streets.

"I believe myself," he thought, "stronger and more logical. Have I denied my old philosophy to such a point? The punishment for laughing at the external world is to fall in the first snare laid by the innocent Maia, as the theosophist expresses it. Could there be, then, an invincible human nature more stable in its versatility than the architecture of thought? Invincible, no, since haughty contemptuous things have conquered it. It is because I lack method. Spiritual training is required. As an elementary precaution, it will first be necessary to place attentive sentinels at the door of the senses, ready to halt every suspected sensation, to admit no one unless stripped of its cloak of deceit....

"Ah! I have no lucidity and I am bored. No remedy, the nervous crisis will accomplish its cycle. It would be somewhat diverting to go to Nice and pierce them with my ironies, but afterwards? Then, the vulgarity of this conduct would be repugnant and hardly fit for a fourth act: then, the case of pistols, the denouement which death hardly saves from a ridiculousness which is bourgeois as well as theatrical....

"Shall I read this letter? I am sure it is full of things which will no longer interest me...."

He stopped and struck the ground with a savage thump of his heel.

"Shame! Enough. No, for me there are neither Circes nor Delilahs. My mind at least is above all wiles and lusts. They who fall into the toils of the swine-breeders, those who are caught in the snares of elegant vampires—they fulfill their destiny. Mine is different. I shall be cowardly neither in facing grief, nor in facing pleasure, nor in facing ennui. You will not make me suffer beyond my will; and neither you, nor any one like you, can tempt me to other disobediences. Even though I be the dupe of my pride, I prefer this to being the dupe of my sensitiveness, and I shall disdain even the memory of the unconscious murderess who might have overwhelmed me."

He entered a café and, developing his brutal bravado to its extreme, wrote, so as to laugh at himself until the blood ran, strange and purposely false verses, which Egyptian readings had suggested to him.

HIÉROGLYPHES

O pourpiers de mon frère, pourpiers d'or fleur d'Anhour
Mon corps en joie frissonne quand tu m' as fait l'amour,
Puis je m'endors paisible au pied des tournesols.
Je veux resplendir telle que les flèches de Hor:
Viens, le kupi embaume les secrets de mon corps,
Le hesteb teint mes ongles, mes yeux out le kohol.
O maître de mon coeur, qu'elle est belle, mon heure!
C'est de l'eternité quand baiser m'effleure,
Mon coeur, mon coeur s'élève, ah! si haut qu'il s' envole.

Armoises de mon frère, ô floraisons sanglantes,
Viens, je suis lAmm où croît toute plante odorante,
La vue de ton amour me rend trois fois plus belle.
Je suis le champ royal où ta faveur moissonne,
Viens vers les acacias, vers les palmiers dAmmonn:
Je veux t'aimer à l'ombre bleue de leurs flabelles.
Je vieux encore t'aimer sous les yeux roux de Phrâ
Et boire les délices du vin pur de ta voix,
Car ta voix rafraîchît et grise comme Elel.

O marjolaines de mon frère, ô marjolaines,
Quand ta main comme un oiseau sacre se promène,
En mon jardin paré de lys et de sesnis,
Quand tu manges le miel doré de mes mamelles,
Quand ta bouche bourdonne ainsi qu'un vol d'abeilles
Et se pose et se tait sur mon ventre fleuri,
Ah! je meurs, je m'en vais, je m'effuse en tes bras
Comme une source vive pleine de nymphéas,
Armoises, marjolaines, pourpiers, fleurs de ma vie!

Following this, Hubert returned to his room, verified some terminologies, and retired.

Tranquilly, by the light of a little lamp, he read Sixtine's letter.

CHAPTER XXXIX

THE KEY TO THE COFFER

Nice,   Friday.
Adieu. This will be a novel without an end, after the modern fashion, for you surely will write it? If not, what is the use? And thus the fugitive shadow will pause an instant and our vain intercourse will have a realization—oh! very relatively—through the creative breath of Art.

Without an end—unless Logic imposes a higher duty upon you.

Without an end,—but I have not the cruelty, knowing you to be devoid of imagination, to let you torture yourself in the vain pursuit of the resolution of the two or three perturbations which my thoughtless words forced on your mind. So I mean to explain the few mysteries—psychological and otherwise—which might trouble the serenity of your mornings.

First, why did I leave? Ah! do not ask it of me, I no longer know why,—but it is irrevocable.

What would you? He captured me. I had to be taken. How often have I not told you that it was necessary to take me and by force and ruse to capture my wavering will? There are such fine strategies that one surrenders, not because of being at the end of resistance, but because the stroke is so well played that it gives pleasure. Ah! you believe women are insensible to Art? At least, this is clear: he captured me.

We were waltzing. He carried me away. "Carry me where you will!"—That was the first submission which—mentally—I made him.

It was toward the hour when the ball's intoxication commenced to evaporate and left me anticipating of the pleasures of sleep. He asked me for the honor (see, nothing premeditated, the honor!) of escorting me home, at the very moment when, wishing to leave, I feared to leave entranced, and find myself alone in the night. I accepted and sent him to call a carriage and await me there. But he discovered that

I was still enjoying myself: he had to wait several hours. Finally, I fled like Cinderella.

I had asked him to wait for me, and he was waiting.

I fear that all this explains nothing, but the result is still more inexplicable. After all, I only wish to vindicate myself of all conspiracy and to convince you of my perfect innocence. It was he, it might have been you,—and I believed that it would be you.

Now, is it my fault? The flower belongs to him who plucks it.

I can now confess to you. Dimly, I loved you.

Ah! that means a great deal! But you did not project any light on this dim twilight. Yes, attempts, trials, approaches, and so on, with which to make a treatise on Analytical Indecision,—and then what? In short, *you* did not capture me!

Why did I not coöperate in the matter? Ah! it is not our feminine habit, and it seems I have already told you that I had been too badly punished for a first choice to make a second one. Now, it is the same as in the romances: By the grace of God! And no responsibility.

(I confess that little was lacking for our enthroning to be effected, but there are moments when the most reasoned reserves become unmanageable. But you urge that you held yourself tranquil until that day, or almost so, arrested at the first sign, disarmed at the first gesture! Do not say that I encouraged you, for you are not ignorant of the fact—you who know women so well—that you must not rely on our encouragements: they are snares, a manner of repetition, to find out, with no peril, how it will take place some day when we shall be disarmed—study the advances another time and see if a mockery is not lodged in the corners of the lips; they are preliminary maneuvers, quite amusing, for even in this child's play we are sure to conquer without alternatives: if our partner grows bold, O power of speech! a word puts him in his place; if he remains cold, we have the consolation that after all we lose nothing thereby, since the conclusion is impossible.)

Before I was eighteen, I married the man of my choice. Well! my great love quickly turned to hate. What caused this change of my sentiments? It would be interesting to know, but even at this hour I do not know its mechanism. I believe I was like the children who want a plaything so much that they cry, stamp their feet, become convulsed with real griefs; as soon as they hold the toy in their little hands, they judge it, thinking: "Is this all it is?" What I had chosen was only this. He loved my flesh and devoured it like an egoist; he uttered immodest pleasantries and debased acts beyond which I felt infinity and the possible unveiling of the ineffable mystery. I thought myself the very creator of Joy and my pregnant desires, my desires big with sobs, miscarried, became the travail of a slave. I knew my destination.

(Imagine! A laughter would seize him afterwards, a nervous laughter which lasted for minutes, a laugh fit to scandalize Hell!)

Yes, I knew my destination and I refused to follow it. Once for all I refused to play the rôle of a bestower of pleasure and a stimulant. I closed my door for ever.

Well, do you know what followed? This monster loved me and could not live without wallowing in my body, in the sun of my eyes. He entreated me, threatened me, turned himself into a slave and dog. I was deaf. Many times we struggled, but in addition to the force of my wrists, which are of iron, I had the force of my will, which is of steel, and I threw him at my feet, trampled upon him, spat on his sex. This endured a year, a long and hateful year.

At last, on the anniversary of the first refusal, he entreated me again, with tears of love in his voice, but with a certain calm that was quite noble. A revolver was pointed to his breast. "No, never!" He fell, and I knew that it was not his fault.

You will find the rest in your memories:

The resolution never again to choose; the resolution to sacrifice myself, in expiation for the first murder, in the event of a second and similar occurrence. I think we have already discussed these two points:

That is all the poison I gave, with an unconscious hand.

(Ah! one day you chilled me so much, in hesitating to guarantee my future. A clear and spontaneous "yes" would have thrown me instantly into your arms.)

Saturday.

This is the legend of the portrait chamber:

Every man who sleeps in this chamber sees, in the course of the first night, the portrait of the woman he must love, reflected in the old greenish mirror. No marriage, no betrothal, no liaison, no oath withstands it: the magical image thrusts itself against the will and it is like a charm.

Could I have told this to you, even laughingly?

Ah! it is not written that the possession will be reciprocated.

I admit that your moon-madness, in which I recognized myself, impressed me. For a long time I believed you were destined to conquer me. The ancient and unreasonable tradition haunted me like a prophecy. If you had only known in what a maze of mystery you courted me! For women willingly curb their caprices under the Fatality which consecrate them as tragediennes. Just fancy! To be the chosen of the centuries and of the dim decrees of necessity! To fall into inevitable arms! To submit to an exceptional law, purposely made for one! It is this which enhances feminity for you and gives a value to the sex.

After all, O analytical romancer, you did not know how to play with anything!

Of course, you will write your novel. Well, I refuse to read it, for it will be full of painful naïvetés. You will naturally glorify your intelligence, your sensibility and your understanding of souls, and also negation, detachment....

Why, then, did you desire me? What phantom did you pursue, if nothing exists outside of your imagination? Yet one should be informed regarding the quality of illusions which one faces. What an alarm in the harem of shadows, among the forms you murdered, bluebeard of the ideal! Have you counted them? I am the seventh, without a doubt, the one who opens the locked room.... "And they passed their swords through his body." Thus Life has killed the Dream. Adieu.

P. S. Besides, you should know that he is not a nobody. Monsieur Renaudeau is going to publish his drama—so moving, so full of genius. He told me this the other evening, at the home of the countess. And this despite you and your gentle contempt, despite you who disparaged him,— without knowing him! After all cui bono.... After all, after all!

CHAPTER XL

ULTIMATE PEACE

"Muchas vezes, Senor mio, considero que si con algo se puede sustentar el virvir sin vos, es en la soledad, porque descansa el alma con su descanso."
Sainte Theresa,
Exclamations of the Soul to its God.

"I was mistaken," Hubert reflected, upon awaking. "This letter is full of interest, but I do not understand this need of railing at me in six small pages. And then to repeat at each line: 'If you had known, if you had been able!' Has she climbed on the stilts of her happiness! Yes, she is happy because a male has thrown himself at her and has nailed her on the cross. Ah! it will be necessary to rise, to carry it, to bend under the burden. Ah! it will bear you down and your lover will mount upwards and stamp his foot on you, for this retaliation is due you.

"Oh! I am not thirsty for vengeance and I do not desire to quench my thirst in the blood which will flow from your severed veins: I do not even wish to see you and I shut you out from my imagination.

"Only.... Ah! the wretch! She does not seem to suspect that I loved her! Everything, under the shelter of passional metaphysics, amounted to a question of adroit and decisive shrewdness. Yes, love is joiner's work.

"And I go into the great absence, but with no mental reservations. I shall not conjure the superficial magics of Claudius Mamertinus; I have perfected them, but I shall use neither those nor my own. The great absence, as one speaks of the great desert, without water and without love! But the Egyptian woman lived there forty years with four tiny loaves of bread which she had bought at Jerusalem; she nibbled at them, when she was very hungry. I, too, shall gnaw at my memories, but not to excess, and without straining for grievous corporeal images. I wish to meditate in peace. Mark you, Sixtine, this is because of my greatness of soul, for I could have carried you off on my shoulders and thrown you into my cavern, where the bones of hyenas, dead of hunger, can be seen. You see that it is not cheerful. So I spare you this exile. Nevertheless, 'you should know what corporeal vision is and you will refrain, when you think of your absent friend, from thinking him really absent. You think of him, and he appears before you corporeally, since you are thinking of his body (and how think of him otherwise, since the body is the sign of his existence and humanity?) And he will rise up before you, and likewise, across all obstacles, you will go into his presence, and he will see you.' And the author of *De Statu Animae* (he also wrote the *Pange, lingua*: he was not a fool), after reflecting, adds: 'Vision is the true function of the intelligent'; and 'the image of things is their true reality.'

"No, I shall, indeed, content myself with little loaves of bread; you will not suffer from my familiarities. In his 'Monitories,' Thomas Aquinas says that too great familiarity begets scorn at the same time that it turns one aside from contemplation and fixes the mind on external things.

"He gives the example of Saint Dominic who, having too affectionate friends at Toulouse, went to live at Carcassonne.

"Well, I do not wish to scorn you under the vain pretext that you have fulfilled your womanly calling, and I wish to meditate in peace, for there remains nothing else for me to do. So, I leave you to your loves and I go to the great desert. Adieu."

Hubert, in turning over his theological books, was already capturing a little of the peace he desired. As long as Sixtine had remained, he had forgotten them for readings more in accord with his perturbations and desires. While putting the two tomes back in their place, he paused in front of this shelf of his library, spelling out the faded letters of gold, surprised at not always being able to guess them correctly. His Origen tempted him: he promised himself to commence the long deferred study of it. Under his fingers, the volume opened on the "Commentary on the Song of Songs," irony of Virgilian fortunes. "His left hand is under my head, and his right hand doth embrace me." But Origen, who remarks that there is everything in this movement of the right hand, "*omnia sunt*," warns against stopping at sensual interpretations. "It is just as well, I am not in the mood for it."

He closed the book and returned to his chair. He re-read the fourth chapter of "The Adorer," congratulating himself on having resolved the supreme fate of Guido according to necessary consequences:

"At least my dream will be logical, as she desires. If life eludes me, transcendency belongs to me. I have paid very dearly for it, I have paid for it with the price of all terrestrial joys. The fruits I bite into are bubbles that soon vanish, but the bubbles which issue from my lips take flight, soar and endure: refracted through them, my ideas, like sun-beams become prismatic, and, with them plays the eternal wind which levels the world.

"In losing you, Sixtine, I have found myself again. But I confess, Madame, that it is not a compensation worth considering. Although you judged me an egoist and although I admit this charge, I bear myself no love. A little hate, rather, when I surmount indifference, for I feel that I am only a bad instrument in the hands of an unknown and transcendental Master,—a Master who laughs so apropos when I abuse my soul.... Destined to what labor? Ah! *he* knows!...

"Tell me, Master! Think of the invincible disgust with which my brothers and sisters fill me! Consider that I need distractions!... O Lord of the gloomy blue meadows where Chimerae browse among the stars, tell me my secret and I shall be capable of true devotion.... Already I love the grace of your saints, for they were alone, deliciously alone:... Often, O Lord, I consider that if anything could sustain life without thee, it is solitude, for there the soul rests in its peace...."

Milton Keynes UK
Ingram Content Group UK Ltd.
UKHW030837021124
450589UK00006B/710